I0889818

GRUBIDO PRESENTS

The ART of FUFU

A GUIDE TO THE CULTURE AND FLAVORS OF A WEST AFRICAN TRADITION

GREENLEAF
BOOK GROUP PRESS

Published by Greenleaf Book Group Press
Austin, Texas
www.gbgpress.com

Copyright ©2021 Grubido

All rights reserved.

Thank you for purchasing an authorized edition of this book and for complying with copyright law. No part of this book may be reproduced, stored in a retrieval system, or transmitted by any means, electronic, mechanical, photocopying, recording, or otherwise, without written permission from the copyright holder.

Distributed by Greenleaf Book Group

For ordering information or special discounts for bulk purchases, please contact Greenleaf Book Group at PO Box 91869, Austin, TX 78709, 512.891.6100.

Design and composition by Greenleaf Book Group
Cover design by Greenleaf Book Group
Interior Pattern Image ©iStock/irinelle
Images used with permission from Amaka Consultant; Charles Richard of Visual Culture; Evomah Communications; Ibehjasper studios; Jeno Uche of Jeno Media; and Taylor Hayden of TMH Creative.

Publisher's Cataloging-in-Publication data is available.

Print ISBN: 978-1-62634-596-6

Part of the Tree Neutral® program, which offsets the number of trees consumed in the production and printing of this book by taking proactive steps, such as planting trees in direct proportion to the number of trees used: www.treeneutral.com

Printed in China

21 22 23 24 25 26 10 9 8 7 6 5 4 3 2 1

First Edition

This book is dedicated to Roosevelt & Safari

Contents

PREFACE // IX

AUTHOR'S NOTE // XIII

ACKNOWLEDGMENTS // XV

1 DESCRIPTIONS OF INGREDIENTS // 1

Meats 2

Seafood 4

Seasonings 9

Vegetables 11

Peppers 17

2 INTRODUCTION TO FUFU // 21

Main Ingredients and Different Types of Fufu 22

Cassava 23

Cassava Fufu 24

Garri 26

Garri Fufu 27

Yam Fufu 28

Yam Flour Fufu 29

Amala Fufu 30

Cocoyam Fufu 31

Plantain Fufu 32

Plantain Flour 33

Semolina Fufu 34

Grains Used to Make Fufu 34

Guide to Fufu Etiquette 39

3 VEGETABLE SOUPS // 43

Edikang Ikong Soup 44
Afang Soup 46
Ofe Owerri 48
Ofe Oha 50
Bitter Leaf Soup 52
Garden Egg Leaf Soup (Ofe Añara) 54
Equsi Soup 56

4 DRAW SOUPS // 59

Okra Soup 60
Ogbono Soup 62

5 WESTERN NIGERIAN SPECIALTIES // 65

Ewedu Soup 66
Obe Efo Riro 68
Gbegiri Soup 70

6 NIGER DELTA SPECIALTIES // 73

Banga Soup 74
Abak Atama Soup 76
Fisherman Soup 78
Nsala Soup 80

7 NORTHERN NIGERIAN SPECIALTIES // 83

Miyan Kuka 84
Miyan Taushe 86
Groundnut Soup 88

CONCLUSION // 91

APPENDICES // 93

A. Main Ingredients and How to Store Them 93
B. Kitchen Equipment 97
C. Testimonials 99

INDEX // 103

ABOUT TheArtofFufu.com // 113

ABOUT THE AUTHOR // 115

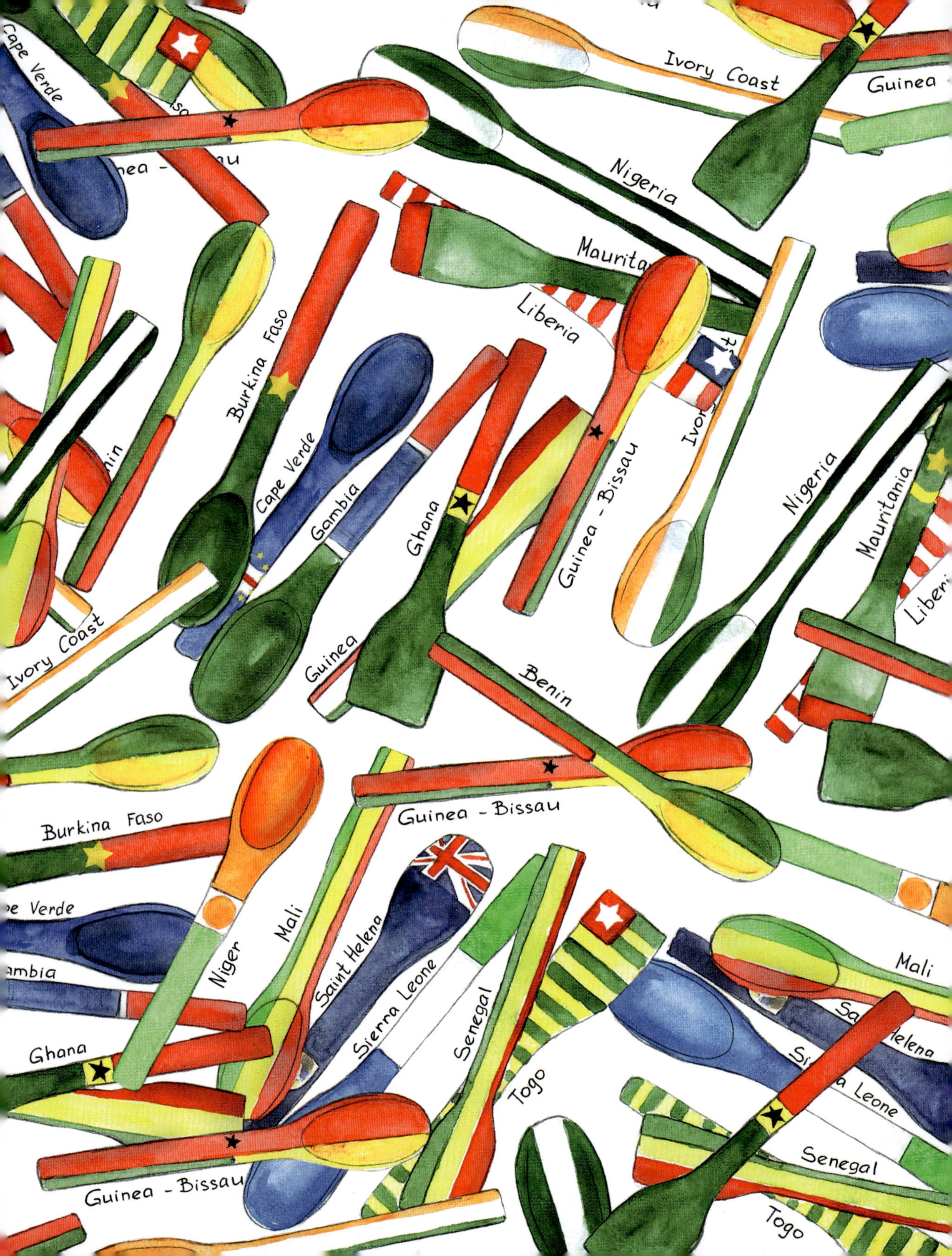
Cape Verde
Ivory Coast
Guinea
Nigeria
Mauritania
Liberia
Burkina Faso
Cape Verde
Gambia
Ghana
Guinea - Bissau
Nigeria
Mauritania
Ivory Coast
Guinea
Benin
Burkina Faso
Guinea - Bissau
Niger
Mali
Saint Helena
Sierra Leone
Senegal
Togo
Mali
Ghana
Guinea - Bissau
Senegal
Togo

Preface

One of the unique aspects of West African culture is its iconic staple food, fufu. A perfect pairing with soup, fufu has a hearty, flavorful character that makes it an essential part of the ideal midday meal to fuel you and keep you energized until dinner. Approach any West African home at lunchtime and the rich scents of fufu will overwhelm you before you even walk through the front door.

Full of tasty, good-for-you carbohydrates, fufu has taken off in popularity. Fufu is native to many West African countries, like Nigeria, Liberia, Ghana, Burkina Faso, Benin, and Cameroon, and is a lunchtime favorite in those countries. And now, it has crossed the Atlantic to fill kitchens in the West with its unmatched flavors and aroma.

In fufu, yam, cassava, yucca, plantain, oats, and other more exotic ingredients combine to produce a soft, melt-in-your-mouth ball of goodness. Fufu is like a large, soft gnocchi—only better. But unlike with gnocchi, you can dip fufu into fragrant Okra Soup, flavored with tasty spices and other vegetables, scooping up the broth with the spoon-shaped fufu.

Or you can capture the taste of the tropics with your fufu when you pair it with Egusi Soup (page 56), which uses the African version of pumpkin seeds that have been sun-roasted and blended with tomatoes, fresh seafood, and hearty vegetables. Dunk your fufu in delicious soups and you're guaranteed a symphony of flavor.

Like many traditional foods, there is an art to both preparing and eating fufu. With few West African restaurants outside of large urban areas, many Americans, and other people throughout the world, may never experience this cultural treasure. As a culinary professional of Nigerian heritage, I want to share this time-honored art—the Art of Fufu—with the rest of the world.

In this book, you'll learn all about the ingredients that you can use to create your own version of this West African favorite, and where you can find them in your corner of the world. You'll learn how important it is to pair the right soup with your fufu, how to make the perfect fufu, how to serve it, and how to eat it with confidence and cultural savoir faire.

Fufu is, after all, an art.

Most important, enjoy yourself as you learn. Don't be afraid to make mistakes. As the West African proverb advises, "Trial and error makes for good food."

That's the Art of Fufu.

"Your food is supposed to be your medicine, and your medicine is supposed to be your food."
—African proverb

Author's Note

This book is an introduction to the flavors and culture of the West African staple fufu. There are different variations of fufu throughout Africa, but in this book, we will discuss the West African region's soups, which provide the perfect complement to fufu.

Many of these soups are Nigerian in origin, since the country comprises a little over 50 percent of the population of West Africa.[1] Though there are numerous tribes in Nigeria, all of which have their own way of making traditional soups to pair with fufu, we regrettably cannot cover them all in one book—there are that many! So for this book, which serves as an introduction to fufu, we are focusing on the more well-known, Nigerian examples of these soups. And because we want our readers to try these delicious favorites on their own, the Nigerian examples are those whose ingredients people are more likely to find in their local grocery stores and can cook in their homes. Also, if you're lucky enough to live in a city with an African restaurant, you're more likely to find these soups on the menu.

Traditionally, the women and men who cook fufu don't measure the ingredients. They cook with their eyes and mouths. They visually check for the right thickness and taste the food while cooking to determine when it is seasoned correctly and ready to serve. With that spirit in mind, know that there are some items for which we may not provide specific measurements in the recipes. For example, you can choose which meats or seafoods you use, and season your soups to your taste. And remember, you can go to TheArtofFufu.com to find more recipes. Enjoy!

---

1 Worldometer, "Western Africa Population," accessed May 26, 2020. https://www.worldometers.info/world-population/western-africa-population/

Acknowledgments

The Art of Fufu would never have come to fruition without the Grubido team, who have worked tirelessly to test the recipes, convert them to standard measurements, research the cultural background of fufu, and finally, write and edit this book. To all those who played a part in the technical aspects of crafting this book—I thank you from the bottom of my heart. This book is a dream come true, and you are my dream weavers.

ACPPB Chapel of Grace
Philip Egwu
Felix Egwu
Funke Sotuminu
Tiwa & Tomi Sotuminu
Bukky Enterprise
Ivy Okoro
Fancy Ezeadun
Dan Fergus
Keke Pitchard
Clevon Timms
Patrick Asadu
Jhayne Udoewa
Patrick Udoewa
Linda Anukwuem
Daniel Adeyemo
Queen Tae
Shakti Baum
Olasumnbo Beluolisa
Stephanie Nwadinobi
Sam Ayeni
Billie Fusigboye
Dr. Alex Haenel
Joy Chibuzo
Crystal choa-choa Chibuzo
Surprise so-so Chibuzo
Ikem Chibuzo Jr.
Charles Capers
Precious Hannah
Courtney Lott
Henry Adaso
Mary Luu Ukegbu
Ashley Ukegbu

1

Descriptions of Ingredients

"Good food is recognized by its looks."
—African proverb

This chapter summarizes some common, key ingredients found in West African soups. You may be familiar with some of these ingredients; others you may have never heard of before.

Palm Oil

Palm oil is a reddish vegetable cooking oil made from the pulp of oil palm fruit. It has a mild, savory, earthy taste used in cooking soups. The African oil palm tree (*Elaeis guineensis*) is native to West African countries.

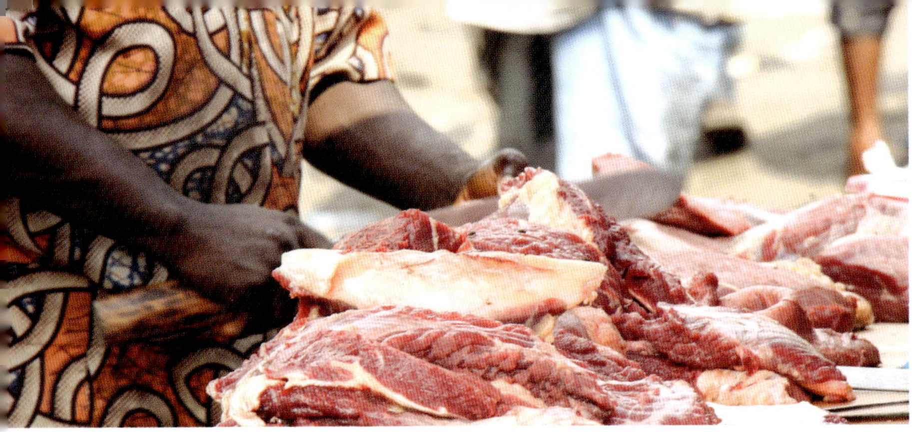

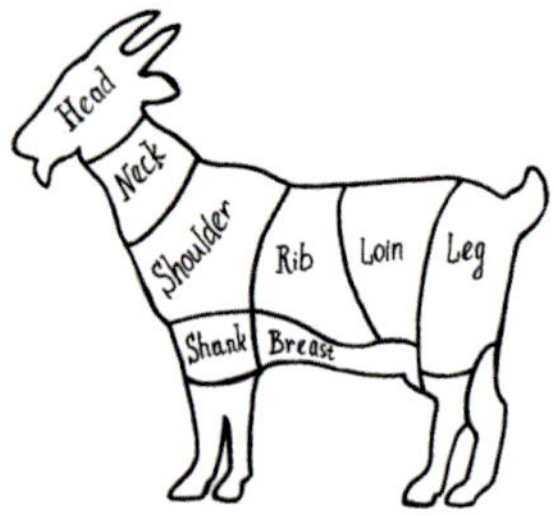

Goat

Hen

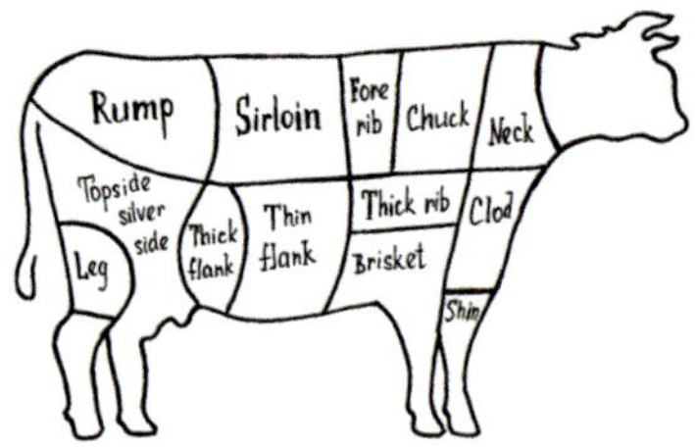

Cow

Meats

Beef

Cows are expensive in West Africa, and beef is served mainly at ceremonies, such as christenings, weddings, or funerals. On these occasions, how many cows the host provides reflects the affluence of the host and their friends. In West African culture, no part of the cow is wasted. We utilize the cow skin, which we call pomo, and the shaki, also known as tripe, the edible lining of the cow's stomach.

Goat

The Nigerian Dwarf goat is a miniature dairy goat breed of West African ancestry. West African Dwarf goats are used in making soups, especially pepper soups. Different parts of the goat are used for the pepper soups, and goat tripe is made from the skull, liver, kidneys, and stomach. It is considered a delicacy.

Goat or ram rearing in West Africa is a business practiced by all tribes, but especially by Northern Nigerians. They rear cattle in large numbers, which gives them the opportunity and capacity to rear goats in large numbers too.

Poultry

African dishes use various kinds of poultry, and they all have different tastes and their own cooking methods. For instance, hen is lean and tough, taking longer to cook, while chicken is more fleshy and tender. In the past, specifically in the 1960s and 1970s, when most families had low incomes, poultry was a staple, and less expensive than goat meat. Now, people also eat poultry at specific holidays or times of the year because of religious or other traditional significance. This is similar to traditions in other parts of the world—for example, eating turkey at Thanksgiving or Christmas in the West. In the last three decades, consumption of poultry has become even more widespread in West African countries, and it is featured in soups and stews throughout the year. Poultry used in African dishes may include hen, chicken, or turkey.

Tidbit

In West African countries, hen gizzard is a delicacy that is as nutritious as it is tasty. In Nigeria, they generally believe that the hen is sweeter than the rooster. This is because the hen is usually older and a local breed. Sometimes the eggs found inside the hen give the meat a unique flavor. The meat is also stronger, providing a much fuller taste.

Tidbit

Which meat is toughest to cook while making soups? The following list details the different meats used in West African soups in ascending order of tenderness, the first in the list being the softest:

- Goat (intestines, liver, kidneys, and stomach)
- Beef tripe (intestines, liver, kidneys, and stomach)
- Goat meat
- Beef
- Chicken
- Turkey

Seafood

In certain West African countries like Nigeria, Ghana, and Ivory Coast, they dry, salt, and smoke fish as a means of preserving a very perishable product. This process is very different from our Western smoked fish, which still need refrigeration. Fish that have gone through this smoking process are tough and need extensive soaking before being used for cooking.

Catfish

African walking catfish are found along rivers and coastal waters. They have a distinctive taste with a mild flavor and you can eat them fresh or smoked.

Crabs

There are many edible types of crabs, which are normally found in shallow ocean waters, such as in rocky pools or coral reefs in Africa. They make for fine eating once you break through their tough exoskeleton.

Crayfish

The biological name for crayfish is *Nematopalaemon hastatus* (estuarine prawn). West African "crayfish" are freshwater prawns or shrimp, and they are not closely related to North American crawfish, which are freshwater lobsters. West African crayfish come dried or smoked, and whole or ground to add flavor to soups.

Dried Fish

Locals eat several varieties of seafood in West Africa. They use dried fish most often when cooking soups. For locals, dried fish or crayfish are go-to ingredients for soups. Having dried fish is a must for good flavor.

In inland streams and on the coast across West Africa, fishermen harvest the abundant herring fish, also called shawa or bonga fish. They smoke-dry these fish over fire for two or three days, and thereafter, over smoldering coals for as long as needed before taking the fish to the market for sale. For the smoking process,

the fish sellers hold the fish with sticks, bars, or wire mesh, depending on the size of the fish. They light a fire on the oven floor and first cook the fish over a high fire. Then, they reduce the fire to a smolder, which they keep going for as long as necessary. Some smoking "ovens" are open and without walls, while others are closed with walls, and they are placed either in the outside air or inside a smokehouse. A hard-smoked herring fish lasts for several months in proper conditions.

Mackerel

Mackerel, also known as Titus fish, is an extremely popular fish in West African countries, and locals use both fresh and smoked Titus fish for cooking. Titus fish is also sold in certain North American seafood markets.

Periwinkles

Periwinkles (*Tympanotonus fuscatus*) are also known as West African Mud Creepers. These are tiny, aquatic snails usually found in brackish water or freshwater in Nigeria, Senegal, Cape Verde, and coastal areas such as Angola. Periwinkles can be purchased with or without shells; when imported from Africa, they come unshelled.

Prawns and Shrimp

Prawns are remarkably similar to shrimp; they are both crustaceans. However, you will find prawns in freshwater, while shrimp are mostly found in saltwater. People across the globe enjoy prawns and shrimp, and they are a popular ingredient in many West African dishes.

Smoked Fish

Originally, smoking fish was a means of preservation. But in recent times, people smoke fish for the unique flavor imparted by the smoking process. Common types of smoked fish throughout West African regions are catfish and tilapia. Catfish is one of the most popular smoke-dried fish in West Africa, the other being mackerel. When the catfish is being smoked, it is customary to pin its tail to its head, and then stake it up to be smoked until it is dry.

Snails

West Africa is known for its giant African land snail (GALS), with two common species found in local seafood markets. *Archachatina marginata* (AM) is found in the forest along the coast of West Africa, mainly in Nigeria. It is often referred to as the "big black snail" or "giant snail." The *Achatina achatina* (AA) is found in Ghana, Benin, Togo, Liberia, and other countries. It is often referred to as the Ghana tiger snail because the shell is similar in color to the tiger and it is found mainly in Ghana.

Stockfish

The fish Nigerians call stockfish is codfish, which they import principally from Norway, especially from Bergen. Codfish is dried for about three months in the cold and becomes extremely hard. It was originally meant only for dog food, but in colonial Nigeria it became a staple delicacy, especially in Southern Nigeria. Stockfish is spreading in popularity throughout other West African countries, adding a unique flavor to enhance soups.

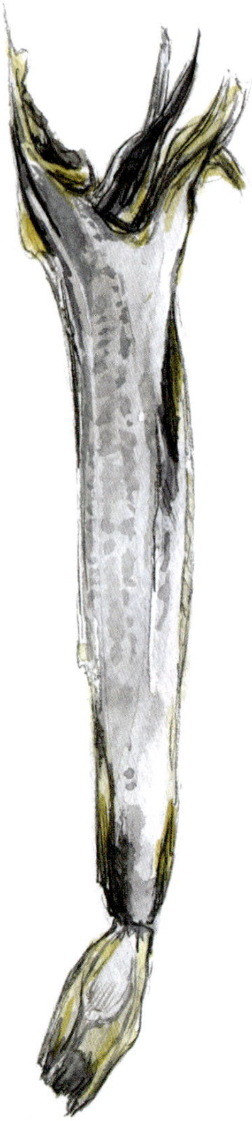

Seasonings

Bouillon cubes

You can buy any brand of bouillon cubes at any convenience or grocery store. They are small cubes of about one centimeter wrapped in light foil. They are made from natural spices mixed with stock, vegetables, and fat.

Ehuru seeds (African nutmeg)

Ehuru (*Monodora myristica*) comes in a hard shell that contains ehuru seeds. Also known as African nutmeg, Jamaican nutmeg, or Calabash nutmeg, it is a less expensive alternative to the mace nutmeg, which is of the same species. The seeds are noted for their aromatic property and in the ground form are used in the cooking of pepper soups, traditional soups, and stews. Ehuru has a strong flavor, so a little goes a long way.

Locust beans

The locust bean, or *Parkia biglobosa*, exists mostly in the wild and primarily in the savanna belt of Africa, spanning the territory from Senegal to Uganda. According to Protabase records, estimates of output range up to 200,000 tons in just Northern Nigeria as of January 2015.[2]

The locust bean spice is made locally throughout West Africa, and, as is common with many of the local food products, goes by different names depending on where you are. It has a strong aroma and is an acquired taste, but it does wonders to the flavor of a variety of soups and stews across the region.

---

2 "Parkiabiglobosa," Protabase record display, cabi.org/isc/datasheet/44162

Tidbit

The Igbo tribe calls locust beans ogiri; the Yoruba, iru; the Hausa, dawa-dawa or daddawa; the Wolof, netetou; and the Manding, sumbala, sunbala, sungala, or sumara.

Potash

Potash is frequently used in the cooking process. Manufactured locally, it is made from plant ashes that are hardened into cubes and are water soluble. In the olden days, this process was conducted in a pot, which is where it got its name.

Uyakay

Uyakay has an outer darkish-brown, smooth-rough bark, and it is botanically known as *Tetrapleura tetraptera*, or Aridan fruit. Aridan fruit hangs on stout stalks and contains a tiny, black-brownish seed. It is a unique aromatic and flavorful spice used in making dishes such as atama, pepper soup, and banga soup.

Vegetables

Atama leaf

Atama leaf (*Heinsia crinita*) gives soup a unique aroma as well as taste. Fresh Atama leaves taste a little bitter and tend to dry up quickly, but they are still good to use in cooking.

Bitter leaf

The botanical name for this popular West African vegetable is *Vernonia amygdalina*, from the family *Asteraceae*. It has differing names by country:

- Fatefata (Nigeria)
- Awonwono (Ghana)
- Ndoleh, njenyani (Cameroon)
- An-gbentho (Sierra Leone)
- Aluma, gbondusti (Togo)
- Bantara burure, dakuna, kossa fina (Guinea)

Ewedu

The Yoruba highly regard the ewedu leaf (or *Corchorus olitorius*), a jute leaf, in their cuisine, principally for soups. Usually, it is cooked separately and then mixed into a larger pepper-based stew. The Hausa people of Northern Nigeria also consume ewedu leaf, where it goes by the name "turgunuwa" or "lallo." The leaf is credited with significant health and nutritional benefits. The jute leaves used for Ewedu Soup (page 66) are packed with antioxidants and Vitamins A, C, and E. They also contain high amounts of calcium, fiber, phosphorus, beta-carotene, iron, thiamin, riboflavin, and niacin.

Garden egg leaves

The cream-colored flesh of garden egg leaves (*Solanum melongena*) has a pleasantly bitter taste (due to the presence of small amounts of nicotinoid alkaloids), and the leaves have a spongy consistency.

Called "añara" in Igbo, garden egg leaves are known to have many health benefits. They are good for pregnant women and kidney issues. The leaves are used for cooking the nutritious Garden Egg Leaf Soup (Ofe Añara) (page 54).

Oha leaves

The oha leaf, or ora leaf (*Pterocarpus mildbraedii*), comes from a tropical tree that grows to a height of up to twenty feet. The broad leaves are pale green in color and are sold as a quite expensive seasonal vegetable. The leaves are used in soups and do not need to be cooked for long. During preparation, they are usually ripped into small bits with the fingers rather than using a knife. The leaves are regarded as a delicacy by the Igbos, and the trees are apparently exclusive to Igboland.

Melon seeds

Melon seeds come from the watermelon species and are dried in the sun, then ground into flour. The flour is commonly used as a thickener for Egusi Soup (page 56) and is the source of the soup's name ("egusi" means melon seed in the Igbo language). Melon seeds and melon seed flour can be found in all the big markets in Benin, Cameroon, Ghana, Nigeria, and Togo. Most cooks mill or grind their melon seeds as soon as they are bought. The powder is saved in airtight containers and stored for future use.

Nchuanwu leaf

Known as African basil, this scent leaf has the botanical name *Ocimum gratissimum*, of the family *Lamiaceae*. It is called "nchuanwu" in Igbo, "efirin" in Yoruba, and "daidoya" in the Hausa language. It is reputed to have numerous medicinal properties, and many even grow it around their homes to serve as an insect repellent.

Ogbono seed

A species of the African tree *Irvingia gabonensis*, bush mango bears the ogbono seed inside. The outer layer is smooth to scaly with a yellow-brown color and a nutty flavor, and is used to thicken soups. Ogbono seeds come from a plant that grows in parts of Africa, which indicates its initial nomenclature classification in the West African country of Gabon. Some people call the seeds dikka nuts, and some others call them African mango seeds.

Palm nuts and palm fruit

Palm fruit is a reddish-brown fruit, about the size of a large plum, and grows in large bunches. These are derived from the oil palm tree (*Elaeis guineensis*), native to West and Southwest Africa.

Pumpkin leaves (ugu)

The pumpkin leaf, or *Telfairia occidentalis*, is a vegetable that comes from a tropical vine commonly called the fluted gourd or fluted pumpkin. It is indigenous to Southeastern Nigeria, principally in Igboland and in the neighboring lands of the Efiks and Ibibio. It is highly regarded for its nutritional and health benefits. The leaves and seeds are both used for making soups. The Igbos call the leaf "ugu," while the Efik and Ibibio call it "ikong-ubong."

Ukazi (Okazi)

The ukazi or okazi orafang leaf (*Talinum fruticosum*) comes from a climbing vine whose botanical name is *Gnetum africanum*, found predominantly in Southeastern Nigeria and Southwestern Cameroon. It is a dark green vegetable that cooks for a long time in soups. It is a staple among the Igbos, who gave it the name "okazi" or "ukazi" and use it for their famous Ofe Owerri (page 48). It is also used by the neighboring Efiks and Ibibios for their Afang Soup (page 46).

Tidbit

Ukazi is known as "eru" or "kok" in Cameroon.

Utazi

The shrub *Gongronema latifolium* is found throughout West Africa. It is a climbing shrub, with leaves that taste sharp and bitter at first and then become slightly sweet as they are chewed. The leaves, seeds, fruit, bark, and roots are all used as food and medicine in the region. Utazi leaf is grown in Southeastern Nigeria and other tropical countries such as Guinea-Bissau, Cameroon, and Sierra Leone. Locally called "utasi" by the Ibibios, Quas, and Efiks, "utazi" by the Igbos in the southeast, and "arokeke" by the Yorubas in the southwestern part of Nigeria. Sierra Leone calls it "ndondo-po-lole," "tawabembe," and "ra-bilong." The Akanakan Asantes from Ghana call it "kurutu nsurogya," and the Seres from Senegal call it "gasub." The herb is reputed to have antioxidant, anti-inflammatory, antibacterial, antipyretic, anti-asthmatic, hypoglycemic, and hypolipidemic properties, and other benefits.

Waterleaf

Waterleaf is a leafy, succulent weed found in waters across West Africa that is thought to be native to Southern Nigeria. It has the botanical name *Talinum triangulare*. The plant grows more prevalently in the rainy season. This fleshy green vegetable has a high water content and is used in cooking soups, especially in Southeastern Nigeria.

Uziza leaf

This is an aromatic vegetable with a spicy, bold taste. The leaf can be pale green when fresh, and darker green when frozen, dried, or blended. Scientific studies indicate that uziza leaves, or *Piper guineense*, are aseptic in nature and can relieve flatulence. They are also useful for treating intestinal diseases, cough, bronchitis, and rheumatism. Nigerians use these leaves to make pepper soup for pregnant women because they believe the leaves set the stomach properly for delivery, stop nausea, and help women after delivery.

Peppers

Alligator pepper

Alligator pepper (*Aframomum melegueta*), or ataeko or atare, is an aromatic seed that has a characteristic fiery taste. It is used for its aroma and believed to have medicinal properties. Merchants sell it whole in pods, and it is a popular ingredient in soups. Said to have antibacterial properties, it is used traditionally to fight coughs and sore throat.

Ground red pepper

Red pepper is used the most in Nigeria and other West African countries; red pepper is the common pepper. This pepper is red when ripe and very small in size. Its botanical name is *Capsicum frutescens*. This pepper is usually ground to powder form and is very hot, much like cayenne pepper.

Negro pepper (uda)

The negro pepper, or *Xylopia aethiopica*, goes by various local names in West Africa. The Igbos call the pepper "uda," the Ghanaians call it "whentia," and the Senegalese call it "Senegal pepper." The plant originated in Africa, but it also is found in South America, principally in Brazil. The fruit looks like small, twisted bean pods, which turn brown after being left to dry for a few weeks. The seeds have a pungent peppery odor and are valued for their health benefits. Whether as seeds or ground, they are popularly used in soups, especially soups for pregnant or postpartum women. Negro peppers possess antioxidant, calming, laxative, and antimicrobial properties. Apart from pepper soups, negro pepper is also used in yam porridge and stews. Together with uziza and utazi leaves, negro pepper (uda) is used in a soup given to women right after childbirth to help with the expulsion of the afterbirth (including blood clots), recovery, wound-healing, and to boost appetite. The uda soup (pepper soup) also helps to resolve various gastrointestinal problems.

Red bell pepper (tatashe)

The variety of red bell pepper eaten in Africa belongs to the species called *Capsicum annuum*. It possesses the deep red color of other red bell peppers, such as are found in markets in the United States, but, in addition, it has an elongated shape, thinner flesh, and a richer flavor. In Nigeria, this red bell pepper is called "tatashe," while in East Africa, it is known in the Swahili language as "pilipili-hoho." Tatashe, as the following pages will show, is a favorite in African kitchens, especially when cooking stews and porridges.

Scotch bonnet pepper (ata rodo)

The ata rodo pepper (*Capsicum chinense*), which is also called the Scotch bonnet pepper, is a variety of chili pepper popular in West African cuisine. Cooks in West African countries who wish to turn out a really spicy dish often turn to the ata rodo pepper, but it is only used moderately because of its spiciness. Ata rodo comes in three varieties: red, green, and yellow, with the yellow being the most spicy and possessing a flavor different from the other two varieties. While the taste of ata rodo varies with the extent of ripeness, the ata rodo has a sweeter taste than the habanero pepper.

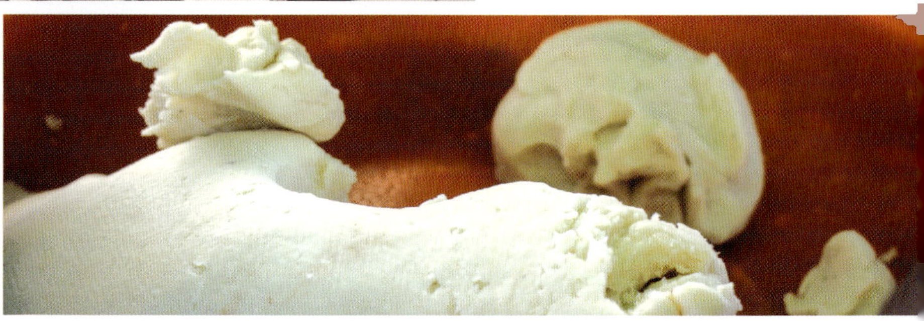

2

Introduction to Fufu

"Interest is the trick of being a good cook."
—African proverb

African culture is rich and vibrant, with an allure of adventure that beckons visitors from other parts of the world. You may come to experience the rhythm of life in Africa. But if you don't get into an African kitchen and learn how to make fufu from scratch, or go to a local restaurant and order an authentic meal, you may not have a genuine story to tell.

Fufu is a staple in West Africa. It is popular in West African countries such as Liberia, Côte d'Ivoire, Ghana, Burkina Faso, Benin, and Cameroon. It is served as a main course and is best consumed at lunchtime because of its high caloric density—it is too heavy for breakfast or dinner. This high-caloric nature is attributed to rich quantities of carbohydrates (up to 84 grams per 100-gram serving). Fufu can be made from ground rice, cassava (commonly known as garri, i.e., processed cassava), pounded yam, processed yam flour, wheat flour, or processed plantain flour.

Fufu is considered an accompaniment to a traditionally prepared soup. In fact, the meal is usually identified by the soup the fufu is paired with (more on soups later).

Tidbit

You may hear the meal referred to as a "swallow" or "eba" meal when you walk into West African restaurants. This is because you don't chew fufu when eating it. It is used to scoop up the soup and is then swallowed.

Main Ingredients and Different Types of Fufu

Fufu can be prepared using different ingredients, depending on where you are from, since different countries grow different crops as staples. The commonly known main ingredients for fufu include the following:

- Cassava
- Garri
- Yam or yam flour
- Cocoyam
- Plantain
- Semolina
- Flour made from grains
- Amala (made from sun-dried yam peels)

Cassava

In West Africa, two types of fufu are developed from cassava: cassava fufu and the more popular garri fufu (which we will discuss shortly). The cassava tuber comes from the cassava plant, which has the botanical name *Manihot esculenta*. This plant belongs to the spurge family *Euphorbiaceae* and is known as yucca and occasionally manioc in South America. It is a woody shrub that grows in tropical and subtropical regions of Africa. Nigeria is now the world's largest producer of cassava. It is one of the primary sources of carbohydrates; thus, it is the major source of food for the local population.

Raw cassava is also a good source of potassium, magnesium, phosphorus, protein, and Vitamin C.

Cassava fufu

To prepare cassava for fufu, you may cut the washed cassava into small cylindrical pieces and soak in water in large clay pots or any other kind of container, preferably located outside, for at least three days. (Alternatively, the containers are sometimes covered with a lid or plastic bag and kept in a warm place.) Storing the cassava this way allows for fermentation to occur—fermentation makes the cassava soft and destroys any toxins in the tuber. Some people also argue that the fermentation adds flavor to the cassava fufu, making it a good pairing for an equally hearty traditional soup. Baking soda may be added to the water during the soaking to help with fermentation.

Tidbit

Fermented cassava has a pungent smell. It's wise to wear gloves while handling it to avoid smelly hands.

During this soaking period, the water is not changed. When the fermentation process is finished, the cassava pieces are removed and peeled (if they weren't peeled before fermenting). Now that the cassava pieces are softer, they are crushed in a sieve, muslin bags, or even cotton pillowcases. The puree that forms is then rinsed with clean water to remove any chaff. The puree will go through the sieve, leaving the chaff behind.

After the sieving is completed, the cassava puree takes some time to dry, and then lime juice is rubbed on it to prevent darkening. Finally, the cassava puree is packed into airtight bags and stored in the refrigerator for future use.

To make cassava fufu, bring the cassava to room temperature and place it in a bowl. Add some water to aid in the binding. Knead the wet cassava flour and roll it into 2-inch balls. Store-bought cassava flour may be sprinkled on the cassava to help with the binding. You may line the bowl with uma leaves (banana leaves are an alternative to uma leaves) to prevent the fufu from burning or sticking (you can cook the fufu on the leaves to avoid it sticking to the pot).

Pour some water into a pot and put the cassava balls into the water. Boil the cassava balls for 5 minutes, until the balls start to crack. Remove the balls from the water, and pound them using a mortar and pestle to get rid of any lumps. This ensures that the cassava balls cook uniformly and prevents the outside of the ball from becoming too soft.

Repeat this process of boiling and pounding twice more. After this, the cassava fufu will no longer be round; it will be flatter and should be off-white in color. A grayish color indicates that the cassava is undercooked.

Cassava fufu is regarded as the most nutritious fufu, especially as it is completely natural with no additives or mechanical processing. However, many families and restaurants in West Africa prefer processed cassava flour in making their fufu. It saves them the hassle of naturally preparing the fufu.

The cassava flour is made into cassava fufu using a process similar to the method used for virtually all fufu made with processed flour. A small amount of water is warmed in a saucepan. The processed flour is gradually poured into the pan and mixed thoroughly in the water using a wooden spatula to avoid lumps. The heat is then increased to medium. The cook continues to stir until the fufu turns from a liquid mixture to a firm yet soft fufu that can be rolled into balls and swallowed with soup.

Cassava flour is rich in carbohydrates, fiber, magnesium, iron, and folate.

Garri

[gah-ri]

Garri, made from cassava tubers, is Nigeria's most common food. It is primarily used to make fufu. The preparer of the garri fufu, usually from the rural areas, peels the cassava tubers, washes them, stacks them in basins, and transports the basins to business owners in the village who operate grating machines. These gasoline-powered machines turn the cassava tubers into a wet rind. The wet rind is sometimes mixed with palm oil. The preparer then fills muslin bags with the cassava rind and then wedges them into wooden straitjackets for three to seven days. These straitjackets act as pressers to remove most of the water while the cassava ferments. This multiday fermentation process must occur before the cassava can be eaten; otherwise, the cassava will retain some toxins, such as cyanide.

After the fermentation process, the bags are opened to reveal cassava that has become dry flour. The flour is fried with palm oil or heated with no oil at all. The oil gives garri a yellowish or light-red color, while those that are fried with little or no oil are off-white. This fried or roasted garri is the final product that is soaked in water and eaten or used to make garri fufu.

Tidbit

Cassava is cultivated as an annual plant with a lifespan of one year.[1]

Garri fufu

Garri is one of the easiest West African foods one can prepare. All you need to do is boil water, pour it in a bowl, and add the garri. Let the garri settle at the bottom of the bowl. This allows impurities to rise to the top and be drained off. To make garri fufu, bring ½ cup of water to a boil in a saucepan, then pour ½ cup of garri flour into the boiling water and stir with a wooden spoon. Gradually add up to ½ cup more of hot water, reduce heat to medium, and stir for about 4 minutes, or until reaching a smooth but thick consistency. You can then use a spatula to form it before serving it with soup, or you can pound it in a mortar to thicken it further.

Garri fufu is rich in calories, carbohydrates, fiber, protein, fat, calcium, and iron.

1 Softschools.com, "Cassava Facts," accessed May 27, 2020. https://www.softschools.com/facts/plants/cassava_facts/1148/.

Yam fufu

While most people eat the more affordable garri fufu, yam fufu is a staple in the households of yam farmers in rural areas.

Other than rural farmers who consume their own yam produce, only the affluent in urban areas can afford fufu made with yam. West Africans delight in eating pounded yam fufu, but they have a greater appreciation for traditional yam fufu made with boiled yam pieces that have been pounded in a mortar until they achieve a smooth, stretchy consistency.

Yam fufu is high in carbohydrates, fiber, copper, and magnesium.

Yam flour fufu

Pounded yam is not readily found in urban areas. However, some households and restaurants still serve pounded yams to their guests. Yam fufu flour is sold in West African markets and international aisles around the world. This processed variety can be ordered in place of pounded yam, no doubt, but the taste and the feel just aren't the same. It should be noted, however, that some West African restaurants do pound their yam in-house because it is a lot cheaper and ensures more natural and nutritious yam fufu.

The preparation of yam flour fufu is quite simple. Warm 2 cups water in a saucepan until it is almost hot, and then add 1 cup of flour and stir with a wooden spatula. (Before adding the flour, you may set aside a portion of the hot water, which could be added later on if the fufu is too thick and not yet done. If the fufu is too watery, you may add some extra flour.)

When the fufu and water have formed a smooth mixture, increase the heat to medium for about 5 minutes. Stir the fufu constantly to produce a smooth, consistent, stretchy yam fufu.

Amala fufu

[a-ma-la]

Amala, derived from yam tubers, is a traditional Yoruba fufu. It is mostly eaten in the south-western part of Nigeria. People who are not Yoruba, being used to fufu's white or off-white color, may marvel at amala's dark brown color. Amala fufu goes wonderfully well with soups such as Ewedu Soup (page 66) and Egusi and Ogbono Soups (pages 56, 62). Traditionally, amala is prepared by peeling and cutting the yam tubers into small pieces and then drying them in the sun. The pieces, which turn brown when dry, are ground into flour. Yorubas call this yam flour "elubo."

To make amala flour fufu, heat some water in a saucepan until it is hot. Begin adding the flour to the hot water and stir continuously until the flour thickens into a smooth fufu. There you go! Your amala fufu is ready.

You can also buy ready-made amala fufu flour. If you are using ready-made flour, follow the directions above. But after a smooth mixture is achieved, increase the heat and cook the mixture for about 4 minutes while repeatedly turning the fufu. This way, you make sure the fufu is heated through.

Amala is rich in calcium, zinc, magnesium, copper, potassium, Vitamin A, and antioxidants, and it has a low glycemic score.

Cocoyam fufu

Cocoyam fufu is prepared in a fashion similar to the preparation of yam fufu. However, cocoyam is rarely used for fufu—mostly, it is used for thickening soups. It also isn't farmed as extensively as yams are. However, the flour is available in most African grocery stores around the world.

Cocoyam is rich in thiamine, calcium, niacin, manganese, Vitamin B, Vitamin C, Vitamin E, copper, and riboflavin.

Plantain fufu

Plantain fufu has rapidly gained popularity among West Africans, as people have become more conscious of the health concerns of consuming too many carbohydrates. To prepare plantain fufu at home, peel and wash 2 unripe plantains. Place the plantains in a blender and process them into a paste. Warm 1 cup of water in a saucepan and set some of the hot water aside in a cup, to add later if needed. Add the blended plantain fufu to the hot water in the saucepan, constantly stirring to mix the water and the fufu mix so that no lumps are formed. Increase the heat and continuously turn the fufu until it's done and ready to be served. You can also make plantain fufu in a microwave. Transfer the blended paste to a microwave-safe bowl, add a little water, mix thoroughly, and microwave the plantain mixture for up to 10 minutes (depending on the quantity of the plantain), pausing the microwave periodically to turn the developing fufu in the bowl so that it cooks uniformly.

Plantain flour

If you do not want to go through the laborious process of making plantain flour, you can buy one of the brands of processed plantain flours that are sold in supermarkets in West Africa, the Caribbean, North America, and Europe.

Plantains are rich in carbohydrates, potassium, Vitamin A, and magnesium.

Semolina fufu

Semolina, which is often used to make fufu in West African countries as well as around the world, is the name of the coarse, processed flour made from durum wheat that is used to make pasta, breakfast cereals, puddings, and couscous. Semolina is not limited to durum wheat, however, as it can also be prepared using other varieties of wheat and other grains (such as rice and maize). Semolina comes from the Italian word *semola*, which means bran—which is itself derived from the ancient Latin word *simila*, meaning flour.

Semolina is full of carbohydrates, packing more than 600 calories in just one cup, making it unsuitable for the diabetic and anyone watching their weight. Cooks usually prefer to serve semolina fufu rather than the traditional cassava fufu or yam fufu because it involves much less work to prepare. Like other fufus, cooking semolina fufu is pretty simple. Warm some water in a saucepan until it's almost hot. Set some of the water aside in a cup. Add the semolina flour to the pot of hot water and stir with a wooden spatula to prevent any lumps from forming. If the fufu is too watery, add more flour. If the fufu is too thick, add some of the reserved hot water. Turn the fufu over and over in the pot until it is heated through and ready to be served.

Semolina is rich in carbohydrates, Vitamins A, E, and K, and thiamine, riboflavin, pantothenic acid, and protein.

Grains Used to Make Fufu

In most supermarkets in West Africa, you can find generic, packaged ground rice, milled wheat, oat flour, and cornmeal that people use to make fufu. The following sections provide more information about the particular grains used to make fufu.

Wheat flour

Many middle-class and upper-class Africans use store-bought wheat flour as their first choice for fufu. However, wheat flour contains gluten, a substance that can cause inflammation in the body and the onset or progression of several debilitating diseases. This is according to a study sponsored by the World Health Organization in 2011 titled "Wheat Flour and Its Diverse Impact on Diabetes" by Dr. John Henry Clark of the University of Ibadan in Nigeria.

Wheat fufu's high glycemic index makes it, despite its pleasant taste and texture, something that people living with diabetes and people watching their weight should avoid. It would be advisable to go for gluten-free flour, if available.

Wheat flour is rich in carbohydrates, protein, Vitamin A, and fiber.

Tuwo

[too-woo]

Southern Nigerians make their fufu with garri, yam, processed wheat flour, ground rice, plantain, and corn flour. However, the inhabitants of Northern Nigeria and the far northern areas of West African countries such as Togo, Benin, and Ghana, where the Hausa and Fulani peoples live, enjoy the tuwo foods. These foods are also a staple in the near-Sahel countries, Mali, Niger, and Chad, where citizens enjoy fufu made with the soft variety of rice meal called tuwo shinkafa. There is also tuwo masara, which is made from corn flour, and the tuwo acha (all of which are discussed in the following sections). Tuwo fufu is enjoyed with Northern Nigerian soups such as Miyan Kuka (page 84) and Miyan Taushe (page 86), among others.

Tuwo shinkafa

[too-woo shin-ka-fa]

Tuwo shinkafa is the most popular fufu in Northern Nigeria and in the adjoining countries of Chad, Mali, and Niger. This fufu is made from rice—the very soft variety that quickly becomes sticky when boiled, like the arborio rice or paella rice used in Northern Nigeria.

To prepare tuwo shinkafa, wash and rinse the rice, picking through it to remove any debris. Put it in a pot over medium heat and add just enough water to cover the rice. Check on the rice frequently to monitor its texture and softness, adding water if needed. Cook the rice until it can easily melt in your hand when pressed. When the rice is sticky, use a wooden spoon to mash it until it becomes a consistent but thick paste. Steam the rice for about 2 minutes, by which time it will be dry. Fold the tuwo into mounds and serve.

Tuwo shinkafa is high in carbohydrates, potassium, and protein.

Tuwo acha

[too-woo a-cha]

Tuwo acha, also known as fonio and "hungry man rice," is cultivated in many countries of Western Africa, including Gambia, Sierra Leone, Senegal, Burkina Faso, and Mali, and in central Nigeria's Plateau State. Tuwo acha is a staple of the Berom people of the area of Jos, in Plateau State. In all the acha-producing areas in Nigeria, farmers tend to dry the newly harvested acha on bare ground; therefore, it tends to come to market with a lot of stones (and sometimes tiny insects). So it is necessary to wash the acha very well and to sift out the stones (in a similar fashion to sifting flour) before cooking.

The rule of thumb for making tuwo acha is to use 2 cups of water for 1 cup of acha. As the water heats in a pot, you must stir continuously while gradually adding the acha. Continue stirring while the pot is boiling to prevent lumps from forming. Once a thick paste is formed, reduce the heat setting to low and cover the pot. (It is necessary to reduce the heat at this point to minimize burning the acha paste at the bottom of the pot.) Cook the acha for 20 minutes. The acha is now ready and can be served with a wooden spoon.

Tuwo acha is high in carbohydrates, fiber, methionine, cysteine, and protein.

Tuwo masara

[too-woo ma-sa-ra]

Tuwo masara is a staple in Northern Nigeria, an original food of the Hausa tribe. It is made from corn flour—the coarse variety of corn flour used in making the corn flour porridge called "pap" or "akamo" by locals. In the northern part of Nigeria, it is common to use this fufu much like garri, pounded yam, tuwo shinkafa, and tuwo acha to eat such soups as Gbegiri

Soup (page 70) and Miyan Taushe (page 86). Some might choose such southern soups as Ogbono Soup (page 62), Egusi Soup (page 56), or Okra Soup (page 60). The Hausa word for soup is "miyan," while the Igbos call it "ofe" and the Yorubas call it "obe."

To make this fufu, use 2 cups of water and 1 cup of flour. Put the water into a pot over medium heat. Gradually add the flour to the water and constantly stir with a wooden spoon. Continue to stir until the mixture becomes thick, somewhat stretchy, and smooth. Add a little more water and then turn the fufu over and over so that it cooks thoroughly. Cover the pot, and let the fufu rest for about 2 minutes before serving.

Tuwo masara is high in carbohydrates, protein, fat, Vitamin B, niacin, fiber, and pantothenic acid.

Methods for Preparing Fufu

YAM

Flour Alternative: YES, YAM FLOUR
Degree of Difficulty: LOW
Regions Primarily Consumed: ALL OF WEST AND CENTRAL AFRICA

PLANTAIN

Flour Alternative: YES, DRIED PLANTAIN FLOUR
Degree of Difficulty: MEDIUM
Regions Primarily Consumed: ALL OF WEST AND CENTRAL AFRICA

CASSAVA

Flour Alternative: YES, GARRI
Degree of Difficulty: MEDIUM
Regions Primarily Consumed: ALL OF WEST AFRICA

AMALA

Flour Alternative: YES, CASSAVA
Degree of Difficulty: MEDIUM
Regions Primarily Consumed: SOUTH AND SOUTHWEST NIGERIA, GHANA

How to Make Pounded Fufu from Scratch

1. Place one small cut piece of boiled yam in a mortar

2. Add all the other cut pieces

3. Pound yam pieces until lumps are removed

4. Once smooth, you can form the yam into fufu balls

Tidbit

A well-done cassava fufu has an off-white color. If it is almost gray, it is overcooked.

5. Pinch the fufu and mold it into a small bowl

Guide to Fufu Etiquette

Fufu has its own eating etiquette and table setup, if it is to be consumed following the West African traditional customs.

Fufu is traditionally eaten using the hands, so you should wash your hands before you begin. This is to make sure your hands are clean; also, the slight moisture on the palm of the hand from the water helps keep the fufu from sticking to your hands.

Fufu is always served with a flat plate and a bowl for the soup. A small basin of water is provided for cleaning the hands. The traditional method is to break up the fufu by hand into bite-size portions (which is the method I recommend). Those who don't wish to use their hands can cut up the fufu into sizable cubes with a table knife. Next, place a piece of fufu in the palm of your hand and roll it into a ball about half the size of a meatball (or whatever size you may be comfortable with). Dip the fufu in the soup using your fork or hand. If you use your hand, mold the ball into a scoop so that you can use it as a spoon to collect the soup from the bowl.

You swallow the fufu ball quickly. Then you sip and savor the soup, chew the bits of vegetable and meat and fish, and swallow—these are yummy moments of an African fufu dish.

How to Roll Fufu

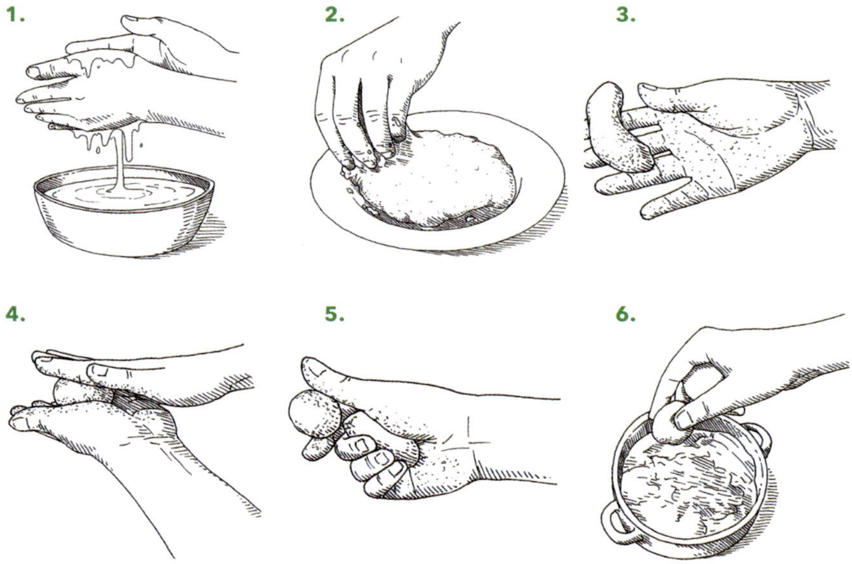

How you decide to eat fufu, with a fork or your hands, is entirely dependent on your personal level of comfort and style. Most of the elite and boarding school students and some fancy restaurants commonly use knives and forks. But it is far more common to see people using their hands to eat fufu. Depending on the consistency, the fufu could be soft or sticky, requiring the periodic soaking of your hands in the basin bowl to get rid of the messy bits of the stretchy glutinous fufu.

Some traditional restaurants furnish a small basin of water and some soap to help diners clean their hands before and after eating fufu. In lower restaurant chains, water is always provided at a nearby tap or in a small bowl beside the food. At these restaurants, knives and forks are not provided, nor are they needed to eat fufu. Generally, many Africans believe that using a knife and fork robs the food of some of its deliciousness. However, if the soup is tasty, you will notice diners frequently and unabashedly licking their fingers.

Essentially, the art of fufu has a lot more to do with the soup than the fufu ball it accompanies. One could say the soup gives fufu its unique taste, as most fufus do not have a great variety of taste by themselves.

When it comes to the preparation of fufu, the process may sound too complex to the uninitiated—until they make their first batch of fufu, which may take only about 30 minutes (unlike the process of making African soup, which can take years to master).

> *"If you wash your hands very well, you can dine with kings."*
> —African proverb

3

Vegetable Soups

"Words are sweet, but they never take the place of food."

—Igbo proverb

Edikang Ikong Soup

[e-di-kan i-kon]

Edikang Ikong Soup is identified by a twin combination of vegetables—the name of the soup itself loosely translates to "waterleaf and pumpkin leaf soup." Depending on a cook's location, vegetables like waterleaf and pumpkin leaf may be hard to come by. However, you may still achieve the delicious flavor of this soup with alternative vegetables like spinach, kale, or lettuce.

Serves 8 to 10

Tidbit

Edikang Ikong is a soup native to the Efik people of Calabar in the Cross River State of Nigeria. The Efik people are, according to legend, descended from the Hebrew people.

INGREDIENTS

2 to 6 cups assorted meats and/or seafood (if desired):

- Beef (including cow foot, pomo, shaki)
- Goat (including tripe/shaki)
- Hen (gizzard)
- Periwinkles
- Snails
- Stockfish
- Smoked or dried fish
- 3 tablespoons ground crayfish

Vegetables:

- 1 large onion
- 1 bunch waterleaves, washed and cut into thin strips
- 2 bunches pumpkin leaves, washed and cut into thin strips

Salt to taste

2 tablespoons ground red pepper

4 cups stock broth

3 or 4 bouillon cubes

5 tablespoons palm oil

PREPARATION

- Wash the meat. (Different meats take different amounts of time to cook, so they might have to be boiled separately. Use the following instructions to cook each type of meat in its own pot.)
- Remove periwinkles or snails from shells and wash, rubbing with lime or lemon juice to remove slime.
- Wash smoked or dried fish with salt and soak in slightly salted water for 5 minutes to loosen any sand or grit. Rinse thoroughly with lots of cold water.
- Put meat in a large pot with just enough water to cover it. Add salt, ground red pepper, bouillon cubes, and sliced onions. Bring the mixture to a boil and cook for 30 to 50 minutes, adding water periodically until the desired tenderness is achieved. Hardly any water should be left in the pot by the time the meat is done. The key is to continuously stir the contents in the final few minutes of boiling to prevent them from burning.
- Add fish and palm oil to the meat pot, and stir.
- Add periwinkles and snails and stir again. Cook for 5 minutes, so the oil and seasonings infuse into the meats.
- Add waterleaves and cook for 3 minutes. Add pumpkin leaves and cook for 5 to 10 minutes. Add additional bouillon cubes or salt, if needed. Stir intermittently to prevent meat from burning at the bottom of the pot. (Stirring this recipe is especially important, as no water is added–the only liquid in the soup is the palm oil.)
- Check the seasonings and serve with fufu.

Afang Soup

[a-fan]

Afang soup is very popular. It originated in Southeastern Nigeria, specifically from the Efik ethnic group in parts of Cross River and Akwa Ibom states. In Cameroon, they call Afang soup "Eru," though Eru is soupier than Afang soup. This soup is usually very thick with the twin vegetables of waterleaf and ukazi leaf. Afang is the Efik's name for ukazi. It grows uncultivated in the tropical regions of Western Africa and is a ready source of a wide array of minerals, including calcium, manganese, and potassium.

Afang soup is revered not only for its rich taste and health benefits but also for its thickness. Unlike other soups that may require added thickeners like beef cubes, Afang derives its enviable thickness chiefly from the ukazi leaves from which it is prepared. One could say that there is no such thing as Afang soup without the ukazi leaf.

The soup is similar to Edikang Ikong Soup (page 44), which is cooked mainly using waterleaves and pumpkin leaves. The tastes of the two soups are strikingly similar, with many people calling the two sister soups.

Serves 8 to 10

INGREDIENTS

2 to 6 cups assorted meats and/or seafood (if desired):

- Beef (including cow foot, pomo, shaki)
- Goat (including tripe/shaki)
- Hen (gizzard)
- Periwinkles (topped and tailed)
- Snails
- Stockfish
- Dried fish
- 2 tablespoons ground crayfish

Vegetables:

- 1 large bunch ukazi/afang leaves
- 1 large bunch waterleaves
- 1 large onion, finely chopped
- 1 Scotch bonnet pepper, finely ground in a blender

3 or 4 bouillon cubes
5 tablespoons palm oil
Cocoyam (optional, for thickening the soup)
Salt to taste

PREPARATION

- In a saucepan, bring a few cups of lightly salted water to a boil.
- Place periwinkles in the boiling water. Cover and cook for 5 minutes.
- In another pot of water, boil meat, snails, onions, and bouillon cubes. Boil until tender, with little water remaining.
- Wash and debone the dried fish. Set aside.
- When meats and snails are done, add dried fish and boil for about 5 minutes.
- Add the palm oil, crayfish, ground Scotch bonnet pepper, and cocoyam.
- As the mixture boils, add the ukazi/afang leaves, along with the waterleaves and the periwinkles.
- When the ukazi leaves are done, add more salt to taste, if necessary.
- Simmer on the stove for about 5 minutes before removing the pot from the heat. The soup is ready to be served. Check the seasoning and serve with fufu.

Ofe Owerri

[o-fe o-we-ri]

Ofe Owerri features ukazi as the main vegetable, although most cooks add pumpkin leaves (ugu). My beloved uncle, Kenneth Ukegbu, was the first to tell me that Ofe Owerri is a "rich soup" because it has everything in it. The Ofe Owerri from Imo State is one of the most expensive Nigerian soups, and here is why: The soup takes a long time to prepare, and the ingredients can be quite costly.

Serves 8 to 10

INGREDIENTS

2 to 6 cups assorted meats and/or seafood (if desired):

- Beef (including cow foot, pomo, shaki)
- Goat (including tripe/shaki)
- Hen (gizzard)
- 6 snails
- 1 whole stockfish, presoaked in water 2 to 3 hours
- 1 medium dried fish
- 2 smoked fish
- 2 tablespoons ground crayfish

Vegetables:

- 4 cocoyams
- 1 large bunch ukazi/afang leaves
- 1 large bunch ugu/pumpkin leaves
- 2 Scotch bonnet peppers, ground in a blender

2 to 4 bouillon cubes
2 tablespoons palm oil
1 tablespoon locust bean spice
Salt to taste

PREPARATION

- Put meat, snails, and presoaked stockfish in their own pots, and add just enough water to each pot to cover the ingredient.
- Boil meat, snails, and stockfish for about 10 minutes. After all are parboiled (partially boiled), combine them in one pot.
- While meat, snails, and stockfish are parboiling, put cocoyam in another pot to boil.
- Add bouillon cubes to the meat, snails, and stockfish. Add water periodically until the meat, snails, and stockfish are done.
- By this time, the cocoyam has softened and cooked. Mash it in a bowl and return it to its cooking pot for later, for thickening the soup.
- Wash and shred the ukazi leaves. Wash and shred the fluted pumpkin leaves, along with the stalk's portion close to the leaves.
- The broth that is left in the meat pot will later be used to cook the soup. Add more water to the pot, and add the dried or smoked fish, ground crayfish, and palm oil. Cook for about 15 minutes.
- Add cocoyam to the mixture. Then add additional bouillon cubes, Scotch bonnet peppers, and locust bean spice, and cook for about 10 minutes.
- Add the cut and washed ukazi and pumpkin leaves to the pot, and cook for about 5 minutes more over low heat. Check the seasoning and serve with fufu.

Ofe Oha

[o-fe or-ha]

Fresh oha leaves are hard to find due to their seasonal nature, unlike most other leaves used in Igbo cooking (which are found on vines and can grow throughout the year). The interesting thing about oha leaves is that while other soup leaves tend to decline in availability during the dry season, oha leaves blossom in the Harmattan dry season. The Harmattan wind comes from the Sahara Desert during the winter months in Europe, bringing very cold air and dust.

The soup is cooked much like Afang Soup, the main difference being the type of vegetables used. Because of its rare quality, Ofe Oha does not take well to substitute vegetables like the other soups we have mentioned. This soup is, therefore, very distinguishable from its counterparts, on account of just one ingredient—the oha leaves used to prepare it.

Serves 8 to 12

INGREDIENTS

2 to 6 cups assorted meats and/or seafood (if desired):

- Goat meat
- Beef (including tripe, cow skin)
- 1 whole stockfish
- Snails
- 1 medium dried fish
- 2 smoked fish
- 3 tablespoons ground crayfish

Vegetables:

- 1 large bunch oha leaves
- 8 cocoyam
- 1 large onion, chopped
- 2 fresh yellow Scotch bonnet peppers

2 to 4 bouillon cubes

4 tablespoons palm oil

Salt to taste

1 tablespoon locust bean spice

PREPARATION

- Start by boiling the meats, beginning with the tougher ones. Once the meat is soft, add stockfish, onions, and bouillon cubes (this will create a tasty broth that can be used later in the cooking). Continue boiling until stockfish is tender.
- Wash and boil cocoyam until soft. Peel and cut the cocoyam, then mash or pound it and set it aside. It will be reintroduced to the soup to thicken it.
- Boil snails in a separate pot. Save the leftover broth.
- Tear the oha leaves into small pieces. (Cutting the oha leaves will cause them to turn dark, and some people claim that using a knife will result in a bitter-tasting soup.) Grind the crayfish and the Scotch bonnet pepper and set them aside.
- Combine the broths and the meat, snails, and stockfish in one pot. Add more water, then pour in the palm oil.
- Add the ground crayfish, bouillon cubes, Scotch bonnet pepper, and salt to taste. Add the mashed cocoyam, locust bean spice, and oha leaves. Cook for no more than 3 or 4 minutes over high heat. Reduce the heat, let the soup simmer for about 1 minute, check the seasoning, and serve with fufu.

Bitter Leaf Soup

When used to garnish Egusi and Ogbono Soups, bitter leaf is washed just briefly, achieving only a slight reduction in the leaves' inherent bitterness. But when used to make Bitter Leaf Soup, the leaves are washed several times and the water is squeezed out of them, leaving lumpy leaves with little bitterness.

Serves 8 to 10

Tidbit

Bitter leaf, in Yoruba, translates to "Adunloun Gbeyinewuro" (sweetness ends bitter leaf).

INGREDIENTS

2 to 6 cups assorted meats and/or seafood (if desired):

- Goat meat
- Beef (including tripe)
- Poultry
- 1 whole stockfish
- 1 medium dried fish
- 2 smoked fish
- Snails
- 2 tablespoons ground crayfish

Vegetables:

- 1 large bunch bitter leaves
- 3 cocoyam

2 to 4 bouillon cubes

3 tablespoons ground fresh red pepper

2 tablespoons palm oil

Salt to taste

PREPARATION

- Peel the cocoyam, then boil it in water until it is cooked. Pound it into a paste using a mortar and pestle, and set it aside.
- Parboil stockfish until tender. In a separate pot, boil beef tripe and meats until tender. Add stockfish, dried fish, smoked fish, and snails to the pot with the meats and their broth.
- Add bouillon cubes, and cook for about 5 minutes.
- Add the palm oil, ground red pepper, ground crayfish, and bitter leaves. Cook for about 10 minutes. Add water periodically to ensure you have enough stock.
- Add the cocoyam paste in lumps in various parts of the pot.
- Cover the pot, and boil the mixture over medium heat, occasionally stirring until all the cocoyam has dissolved.
- Add water if the soup is too thick. Add salt to taste.

Garden Egg Leaf Soup (Ofe Añara)

[o-fe] [a-ña-ra]

Ofe añara are garden egg leaves, which are best used when freshly plucked from the garden. Slightly dried leaves may be the only ones available away from the farms and markets in rural areas. They may not have the same delicious taste as the fresh ones. The leaves have a slightly bitter taste, but this adds to their popularity with people who may have illness-induced nausea. The soup is also great for people watching their weight or battling to keep their blood sugar in check.

Serves 8 to 10

INGREDIENTS

2 to 6 cups assorted meats and/or seafood (if desired):

- Goat meat
- Beef
- Hen
- 1 whole stockfish
- 1 medium dried fish
- 2 smoked fish
- 2 tablespoons ground crayfish

Vegetables:

- 3 cocoyam
- 1 bunch garden egg leaves
- ⅓ cup palm oil

2 to 4 bouillon cubes

1 tablespoon locust bean spice

Salt and pepper to taste

PREPARATION

- Parboil the stockfish in water, together with the cocoyam, with a bouillon cube added for flavor if desired.
- Wash and debone dried fish and smoked fish in warm water.
- When cocoyam is done, remove it from the stockfish pot and pound it to a paste.
- Add water periodically to stockfish pot and keep cooking until stockfish is soft.
- Remove stockfish from the pot and set it aside.
- Put the dried and smoked fish, various meats, and bouillon cube (if using) into the pot. Bring the mixture to a boil.
- When the meat and fish are done, put the stockfish back into the pot and add the palm oil, cocoyam paste, crayfish, locust bean spice, and pepper. Add a minimal amount of salt. The taste of this soup is slightly bitter by design.
- Finally, add the washed and cut garden egg leaves. Cook for only about 3 minutes, which is just enough time for the vegetable to impart its unique flavor to the soup. Remove the soup from the heat and serve.

Egusi Soup

[e-gu-si]

Egusi Soup is now cooked and eaten all over West Africa. In the Hausa language, the soup is called "Miyan Gushi." In Ghana, it is called "Agushi." It is referred to as "Obe Efo Elegusi" in Yoruba. Among the Yorubas, vegetables are not normally included in this soup, but among the Igbos and their neighbors, fresh chopped okazi (also called "ukazi," "eru," and "afang") or ugu (fluted pumpkin leaves) are added. Alternatively, they also use dried bitter leaf, which adds a slightly bitter taste to the soup—something that may be necessary for some palates.

Serves 7 to 10

INGREDIENTS

2 to 6 cups assorted meats and/or seafood (if desired):

- Beef (cow foot, pomo, shaki/tripe)
- Goat
- Hen (gizzard)
- Dried fish
- Stockfish
- Snails
- 4 tablespoons ground crayfish

Vegetables:

- 2 fresh peppers (any variety), chopped
- 1 large onion
- 1 bunch vegetables (such as pumpkin leaves, bitter leaf, or okazi)
- 4 cups ground melon seeds (egusi)
- Chopped tomatoes, for garnish

⅓ cup palm oil (plus more for cooking vegetables)

1 tablespoon locust bean spice

2 bouillon cubes

Salt to taste

PREPARATION

- Before you begin preparing the soup, note that the dried fish is normally soaked for at least 30 minutes to soften it and help clean it very well. Meanwhile, the stockfish is usually soaked overnight or cooked with a pressure cooker since it takes a long time to soften it through boiling.
- Blend the peppers and onions. Put some oil in a pot, and add the blended peppers, onions, and crumbled bouillon cubes. Cover the pot, and cook the mixture for about 2 minutes.
- Add meat, dried fish, stockfish, and ground crayfish, and cook for 10 minutes. (If you are using meat, wash and cook it separately before being added here. The meat stock can also be poured into the soup mixture to give it an added flavor. If you are using beef tripe, wash it and cook it in a separate pot over medium heat with some sliced onions, 1 or 2 bouillon cubes, and salt and pepper.)
- After the fish are done, debone all the fish except the stockfish, and set aside. Remove the beef and beef tripe from the pots in which they were cooked. Leave the water used to cook the meat and fish in their respective pots.
- Wash the vegetables (such as pumpkin leaves, bitter leaf, and okazi), cut them into little pieces, and set them aside.
- The next step is to begin introducing the ground egusi into the pot that contains the meat and fish's cooking water. Cover the pot, but stir frequently to prevent the mixture from sticking, adding a little more water if necessary.
- After about 25 minutes, you should see the oil from the egusi rising to the soup's surface. At this point, add palm oil, the washed and cut vegetables, locust bean spice, crayfish, and salt to taste. Cook for 7 minutes.
- As the soup turns a light yellow color, add the various meats and seafood. Stir the soup and let it simmer for 5 minutes.
- Garnish the soup with tomatoes and serve.

Tidbit

The egusi in the soup provides some reported antidiabetic effects, which should be considered beneficial, considering the starch in the fufu.

4

Draw Soups

"No matter how hot your anger is, it cannot cook yams."

—Nigerian proverb

Okra Soup

Okra Soup is arguably one of the quickest soups to prepare. The vegetables might require some time and care, but once they are ready, the soup will cook in no time. You may choose to mix it with some ogbono, as some do. In this instance, all you have to do is add the okra to the ogbono. However, you can vary the ratio of ogbono to okra depending, of course, on which you want more of in the soup.

Okra is a favorite among West African children, including those raised overseas in North America and Europe. So mothers will be especially fond of it because it is so nutritious and easy for children to eat. It is a starter meal for toddlers who are ready to start their foray into adult food—there is no worthier introduction. Perhaps okra appeals to children so much because of its gelatinous quality, which makes it easy to swallow and finish—especially with youngsters who want to be done with their food quickly so they can head outside to play.

In West Africa, Okra Soup is called "draw soup," because it tends to be elastic. We don't want to use the more descriptive word—gelatinous. There is nothing slimy (that is, disreputable) about Okra Soup; it is a very delicious soup. Maneuvering it can be quite messy, however, as it easily slips over the bowl and lands on the table. It requires constant use of a napkin because it also easily runs down your chin from your mouth. For beginners in the art of eating fufu with Okra Soup, it is advisable not only to keep a napkin handy but also to tuck a napkin into the front of your shirt to prevent stains. Okra is low in calories but contains high levels of essential vitamins and minerals, such as Vitamins A, B1, B2, B6, C, and folic acid. Okra also contains riboflavin and dietary fiber, along with traces of calcium, zinc, and potassium. Its content of folic acid and minerals makes it ideal for eating during pregnancy.

Serves 8 to 10

Tidbit

Okra is also known as "lady fingers"–"Miyan Kubewa" in Hausa; "Ofe Okwuru" in Igbo; and "Obe Ila" in Yoruba.

INGREDIENTS

2 to 6 cups assorted meats and/or seafood:

- Beef (cow foot, pomo, shaki/tripe)
- Goat
- Hen (gizzard)
- 1 whole stockfish (pieces)
- 1 medium dried fish
- 2 smoked fish
- 3 tablespoons ground crayfish

Vegetables:

- 30 okra pieces or 5 cups chopped
- 1 large onion, chopped
- 1 large bunch pumpkin leaves, washed and cut into small pieces
- 2 fresh yellow Scotch bonnet peppers

1 tablespoon ground red pepper
2 to 4 bouillon cubes
½ cup palm oil
1 tablespoon locust bean spice
Salt to taste

Note: The words "ofe," "obe," and "miyan" are the respective Igbo, Yoruba, and Hausa equivalents of the English word "soup."

PREPARATION

- Wash okra and split into two portions. Puree one portion in a blender; the other should be finely diced, to add to the soup later.
- If you want to achieve a reasonable amount of draw, then you must be very careful about how you cut and prepare the okra for cooking. You must cut the okra pods into very tiny pieces, mixing up horizontal and vertical cuts.
- To prepare soup, soak stockfish and dried fish beforehand, until tender (about 15 hours). The stockfish will also need to be precooked; see below.
- Combine crayfish and ground red pepper.
- Wash and debone dried fish.
- Boil beef tripe, if using, and stockfish in the same pot until they are soft.
- Add various meats, onions, bouillon cubes, and ground crayfish-pepper mixture. When meat is tender, add dried fish.
- Put palm oil in another pot and heat it. When oil becomes hot, add pureed okra and fry it.
- Add some of the water left from boiling the beef and fish. Within about 5 minutes, the okra will be cooked and will have started to "draw." At this point, add pumpkin leaves, remaining diced okra, meats, fish, crayfish, locust bean spice, peppers, and salt.
- Cover the pot and allow the soup to simmer for about 15 minutes.
- Stir the soup intermittently.
- Check the seasoning and serve with fufu.

Ogbono Soup

[o-gbo-no]

The Igbo people of Southeastern Nigeria treasure this soup and gave the ogbono seeds their name. Ogbono Soup is the quintessential draw soup, along with Okra Soup (page 60). The two soups are so described because of their elasticity and tendency to drip off the mouth and bowl. People eating fufu with Ogbono Soup typically use their hands. Using a spoon to scoop the soup into the mouth can be challenging, as a lot of the soup will fall off the spoon back into the bowl or onto the table. Also, most diners just want the quantity of soup that sticks to the ball of fufu after the latter is dipped in the soup bowl; they don't want the larger quantity of soup that a spoon would provide.

Using ogbono seeds not more than three months old will make for a good soup. And it is also essential to keep the seeds or their powder in airtight containers (or, if possible, keep them refrigerated to maintain their freshness if you plan to use them later).

The nutritional benefits of Ogbono Soup and ogbono seeds receive a lot of attention. Ogbono is said to increase the levels of adiponectin, a protein thought to help the body regulate blood glucose levels and decrease cholesterol. Africans have eaten these seeds in one form or another for hundreds of years; they surely knew without understanding that ogbono seeds were good for their bodies. The high fiber content of ogbono seeds is said to contribute to its health benefits.

Serves 8 to 10

Tidbit

Ogbono has been featured on *The Dr. Oz Show*, where it was reported to have significant health benefits, especially for weight loss and for the decrease of blood glucose and bad cholesterol.

INGREDIENTS

2 to 4 cups assorted meats and/or seafood:

- Beef (cow foot, pomo, shaki/tripe)
- Goat
- Hen (gizzard)
- 2 cups periwinkles
- 4 snails
- 1 large dried fish
- Stockfish
- 2 tablespoons dried crayfish

Vegetables:

- 1 large onion, chopped
- 2 fresh tatashe peppers, chopped
- 1¼ cups ground ogbono
- ½ bunch bitter leaves or ½ bunch pumpkin leaves

3 to 4 bouillon cubes, divided
⅓ cup palm oil
1 tablespoon locust bean spice
Salt to taste

PREPARATION

- Wash assorted meats thoroughly and place them in a pot with enough water to cover them.
- Boil meat with onions, peppers, salt, and 2 or 3 bouillon cubes. (This procedure adds flavor to the meat, and the resulting broth will be used later in cooking the soup.)
- Boil periwinkles and snails in salted water, then wash them carefully. (Like beef tripe, snails take a long time to cook.)
- Wash dried fish with warm water, and debone.
- Add stockfish, dried fish, crayfish, and locust bean spice to meat cooking broth and allow to cook for 10 minutes.
- In another pot, heat palm oil and fry ground ogbono seeds for 3 minutes to bring out the nutty flavor.
- Gradually add stock and whisk until it draws and bubbles. Then, add the cooked meats, fish, snails, periwinkles, and peppers.
- After about 5 minutes, add pumpkin leaf or bitter leaf and 1 bouillon cube, and boil for another 3 minutes. Check the seasoning and serve with fufu.

5

Western Nigerian Specialties

"Trial and error produces good food."
—Anonymous

Ewedu Soup

[eh-weh-du]

Ewedu Soup is made of a green vegetable preparation combined with meat or fish stew. Stew is added to cook the soup, and Yoruba people enjoy cooking this soup because most of them will use an ewedu broom to whisk the ingredients. However, we are in luck: We can use the blender to puree the ewedu leaves. The ewedu itself is made of jute leaves (*Corchorus olitorius*), which are also called ewedu leaves.

Serves 2 to 5

INGREDIENTS

Vegetables:

- 1 bunch ewedu or jute leaves, washed and ground in a blender
- 1 large onion
- 2 fresh tatashe peppers

4 to 5 tablespoons ground crayfish

1 tablespoon locust bean spice

1½ cups stock water

1 bouillon cube

1 tablespoon potash

Salt to taste

PREPARATION

- Combine ground crayfish, locust bean spice, and ground ewedu leaves.
- Put this mixture in a pot with 1½ cups stock water over medium heat. Add crumbled bouillon cube, potash, and salt to taste. Do not cover the pot throughout this procedure. Boil for 2 to 3 minutes.
- When Ewedu Soup is ready, mix it with separately cooked meat or fish stew. Check the seasoning and serve with fufu.

Obe Efo Riro

[o-be e-fo ri-ro]

Obe Efo Riro is a very popular Yoruba soup/stew in Nigeria. The name "efo" means vegetables; hence, it is rich in vegetables. It is similar to Edikang Ikong Soup (page 44). Enjoy Efo Riro savory spinach soup as a vegetarian dish or with the option of adding meat or fish.

Serves 5 to 8

INGREDIENTS

Assorted meats and/or seafood (if desired):

- Beef (cow foot, pomo, shaki/tripe)
- Goat
- Hen
- 4 tablespoons ground crayfish
- Dried fish
- Stockfish
- Snails
- Mackerel

Vegetables:

- 2 bunches spinach, washed
- 1 large onion, chopped
- 1 large red bell pepper, chopped
- 2 Scotch bonnet peppers, chopped

⅓ cup palm oil

1 tablespoon locust bean spice

4 bouillon cubes, divided

4 cups stock broth

Salt to taste

PREPARATION

- Heat a little water in a pot. Add a crumbled bouillon cube and let it dissolve in the water. Then add spinach and cook it for 1 minute. Drain off the water and set cooked spinach aside.
- Make the base sauce by blending onion, bell pepper, Scotch bonnet peppers, and locust bean spice to produce a chunky mixture.
- Heat palm oil in a pot and add the blended mixture. Now, add 2 crumbled bouillon cubes and periodically stir the mixture. After the pot has boiled for about 10 minutes, add ground crayfish and continue boiling. Add salt to taste.
- Add the various precooked meats/seafood and cook for an additional 5 minutes, stirring to mix the ingredients together. Then cover the pot and let simmer for another 5 minutes. Add another bouillon cube, followed by the blanched spinach, and cook for another 5 minutes.

Gbegiri Soup

[gbe-gi-ri]

Gbegiri soup is one of the traditional staple soups in the western part of Nigeria. Gbegiri means "beans" in the Yoruba language. It is a very simple soup to make. This soup originates from Oyo State.

Serves 2 to 5

INGREDIENTS

Vegetables:

- 2 cups black-eye beans
- 1 medium onion, minced

1 tablespoon potash
⅓ cup palm oil
3 tablespoons ground crayfish
2 bouillon cubes
2 tablespoons ground pepper
1 tablespoon locust bean spice
Salt to taste

PREPARATION

- Wash and peel skins of black-eye beans.
- Boil beans in a saucepan of water and add potash. When beans are sufficiently softened, drain and mash them.
- Add palm oil to the mashed beans and heat the mixture until it turns yellow. Add minced onions, crayfish, bouillon cubes, pepper, and locust bean spice.
- Simmer for an additional 3 minutes, and the soup is ready. Check the seasonings and serve with fufu.

6

Niger Delta Specialties

"One spoon of soup in need has more value than a pot of soup when we have an abundance of food."
—Anonymous

Banga Soup

Delta people, with whom Banga Soup is most associated, cook the Banga Soup either without any vegetables at all, or they use dried and crushed bitter leaf vegetables.

One thing to note about Banga Soup is the palm oil. It is not the regular pure palm oil extracted from ripe palm fruits at high temperatures. Instead, it is the extract that comes from the same palm fruit pulp at low temperatures, which is mixed with water.

Serves 8 to 12

INGREDIENTS

2 to 6 cups assorted meats and/or seafood:

- Beef (cow foot, pomo, shaki)
- Goat (tripe)
- Hen (gizzard)
- 1 fresh fish
- 1 large dried fish, washed and deboned
- 1 medium stockfish, washed and parboiled
- 4 tablespoons dried crayfish

Vegetables:

- 800 grams tinned palm fruit concentrate
- 1 large onion, sliced
- 1 bunch dried bitter leaf, washed and chopped

2 bouillon cubes, divided
2 tablespoons ground pepper
Salt to taste
2 tablespoons locust bean spice

PREPARATION

- Place the meat or fresh fish in a large pot and cover with water. Add sliced onions, 1 bouillon cube, ground pepper, and salt. Cook until tender.
- Add dried fish and parboiled stockfish to boiled meat and cook for 5 minutes.
- Add crayfish and locust bean spice.
- Pour about a cup of the stock water (reserving 1 cup for later) into a blender, adding onion, crayfish, and locust bean spice.
- Transfer the contents of the blender to a pot, and add the palm fruit concentrate to the ground spices.
- Heat the spices and oil mixture.
- Add meat/fish, another 1 cup of stock water, 1 bouillon cube, and stir.
- Allow mixture to boil until soup is slightly thick.
- Add bitter leaf, cover the pot, and let simmer for about 5 minutes. Check the seasoning and serve with fufu.

Palm Nuts

Abak Atama Soup

[a-bak a-ta-ma]

Atama Soup, named after the people of Abak, is a Niger Delta delicacy that features periwinkles (or baby snails). The atama leaves are very aromatic, which gives the soup a rich smell as well as a distinct flavor. Atama leaves provide flavonoids and phenolic antioxidants.

Serves 2 to 5

INGREDIENTS

2 to 6 cups assorted meats or seafood:

- Beef (shaki, pomp, tripe)
- Goat
- Hen
- Stockfish
- 2 cups periwinkles
- 1 fresh fish
- Shrimp
- 4 tablespoons dried crayfish
- Stockfish

Vegetables:

- 400 grams tinned palm fruit concentrate
- 1 bunch atama leaves, washed and cut into small pieces
- 1 tablespoon uyayak
- 1 onion, chopped
- 2 tatashe peppers

Salt and pepper, to taste

3 bouillon cubes, divided

PREPARATION

- Cut the meat into pieces and season it with salt and pepper. In a pot of water over low heat, boil the meat with 2 bouillon cubes and chopped onions for about 5 minutes. Add more water (if necessary) and the head of the stockfish to the pot and boil for an additional 20 minutes.
- When meat is cooked, remove the pot from the heat.
- Pour palm fruit concentrate into a pot and let it heat on the stove for about 5 minutes to remove all moisture. Add the hot palm fruit concentrate to the pot containing the seasoned meat and fish in its stock. Also add the washed/deboned fresh fish, periwinkles, shrimp, dried crayfish, uyayak, 1 bouillon cube, salt, and tatashe pepper and boil the mixture for 10 minutes.
- Add atama leaves and boil another 10 minutes, stirring occasionally.
- Simmer soup for another 10 to 15 minutes, or until it thickens. Remove from heat and check seasoning. Serve with fufu.

Fisherman Soup

Fisherman Soup is native to Nigeria's Rivers State and Cross River State. Fisherman Soup is a very simple soup to make and cooks pretty quickly. It probably came into vogue in riverine areas of Nigeria. When the fishermen returned home with their catch, it was easy for their wives and mothers to get a selection of fresh fish. They could prepare something fast and delicious that also satisfied their hunger.

Serves 8 to 10

INGREDIENTS

2 to 6 cups assorted seafood:

- Fresh fish (such as croaker or monkfish)
- Periwinkles
- Clams without shell, cleaned
- Crabs
- Tiger prawns
- Dried fish
- Lobster
- Mussels
- Smoked fish
- 3 tablespoons ground crayfish

Vegetables:

- 1 bunch pumpkin leaves, washed
- 1 onion, chopped
- 1 red bell pepper, chopped
- 1 bunch basil leaves, sliced
- 10 okra, chopped
- 2 tatashe peppers, sliced

3 or 4 bouillon cubes

4 tablespoons palm oil

2 tablespoons cocoyam

Salt to taste

PREPARATION

- Combine onions, red bell peppers, and fresh basil leaves. Add the mixture to a pot of water and bring it to a boil.
- Add fresh fish, dried fish, and ground crayfish, and allow the mixture to cook for about 5 minutes.
- Add okra, tatashe peppers, and bouillon cubes, and cook for an additional 5 minutes.
- Add palm oil to the pot and cook for another 5 minutes. Add pumpkin leaves and boil for up to 7 more minutes. Add cocoyam thickener and cook for 5 more minutes.
- Check the seasoning and serve with fufu.

Nsala Soup

[In-sa-la]

Also known as White Soup because of its light color, Nsala Soup is eaten mostly in Southeastern Nigeria. The palm oil that goes into most soups is omitted in this dish. Catfish is a key ingredient, although if this species of fish is unavailable, conger eel and periwinkles are good substitutes. Meat and dried fish are also used.

Serves 8 to 10

INGREDIENTS

2 to 4 cups assorted meats or seafood (optional):

- Beef (cow foot, pomo, shaki/tripe)
- Goat
- Hen
- Fresh catfish
- Dried fish (optional)
- Stockfish (optional)
- 2 tablespoons ground crayfish

Vegetables:

- 2 medium sliced yams
- 1 small bunch uziza leaves, washed and shredded
- 1 medium onion, chopped
- 2 fresh peppers, chopped

2 tablespoons locust bean spice
3 bouillon cubes
Salt to taste

PREPARATION

- Boil the yam pieces thoroughly; drain. Pound them in a mortar or process them in a blender. Set the yam aside.
- Cut uziza leaves into tiny shreds. Blend the crayfish and chopped peppers and set aside.
- Cut catfish into 1-inch-thick pieces and remove the intestines. Place in a bowl. Pour hot water over the fish pieces to remove the slimy substance of the outer skin. (Hot water also toughens the flesh to prevent it from breaking apart when cooking the soup.) Leave for 2 minutes, then rinse with cold water.
- Place catfish in a pot with 4 cups of water to heat. Add onions, peppers, locust bean spice, bouillon cubes, and salt. When the preceding ingredients have been cooked sufficiently, add uziza leaves. Also add yam paste in small lumps.
- Cover the pot and allow the contents to cook over medium heat until all the yam paste has dissolved. While cooking, if you think that the yam paste will make the soup too thick for your taste, you can remove some paste that has not dissolved.

7

Northern Nigerian Specialties

"Knowledge is like a garden;
if it is not cultivated, it cannot be harvested."
—Anonymous

Miyan Kuka

[mi-yan ku-ka]

Known also as Luru Soup, Miyan Kuka takes its name from the dried leaves of the baobab. The baobab tree grows all over Northern Nigeria as well as farther north in Niger, Mali, Chad, and across the Sahara to Sudan and beyond to the Maghreb (Arab North Africa). The baobab leaves, when prepared for food, are called "kuka." The Hausa and their neighbors prepare the Miyan Kuka or Luru Soup with the tree leaves as well as dried okra. The baobab leaves are dried and then powdered. In restaurants and homes in Hausa-speaking areas of West Africa, most diners eat their tuwo fufu and Luru soup with their hands. One other thing to note: Miyan Kuka tends to taste better the day after it is cooked.

Serves 8 to 10

INGREDIENTS

1 to 2 pounds assorted meats:

- Goat meat
- Beef (tripe, shaki, or pomo)
- Chicken

Assorted seafood:

- 1 large dried fish
- 3 tablespoons ground crayfish

Vegetables:

- 1 onion, chopped (plus more to season beef stock, if desired)
- 2 fresh tatashe peppers
- 4 fresh tomatoes
- 1 cup kuka powder (dried baobab leaves)
- 1 cup dried, ground okra

1 or 2 bouillon cubes

1 tablespoon locust bean spice

4 tablespoons palm oil

Salt to taste

PREPARATION

- Wash beef and place in a pot of water. Add chopped onions and salt to taste. Allow the beef to boil till slightly tender, about 30 minutes.
- Place dried fish in a bowl of hot water to soak for a few minutes to kill off any impurities.
- While the beef cooks, put 2 cups of water in a blender; add the peppers, onions, tomatoes, ground crayfish, and locust bean spice.
- After the beef has cooked for 30 minutes, add dried (soaked) fish, palm oil, and bouillon cubes. Add enough water to reach your desired consistency. Then gradually add the locust bean spice paste to the pot, stirring all the while so that the paste mixes smoothly with the water and does not become lumpy. Cook for another 30 minutes.
- Remove beef, bones, and dried fish and set them aside. Add powdered kuka leaves and okra to the pot, a pinch at a time, to ensure they mix smoothly with the soup and do not make the soup lumpy (add water if needed). Transfer beef and fish back to the pot. After about another 15 minutes of boiling, the soup is ready. Check the seasoning and serve with fufu.

Miyan Taushe

[mi-yan tau-sheh]

Enjoyed with tuwo shinkafa fufu, Miyan Taushe is a treasured Northern Nigerian soup.

Serves 10

INGREDIENTS

1 to 2 pounds assorted meats:

- Goat meat
- Beef (tripe, shaki, or pomo)
- Chicken

Assorted seafood:

- 1 medium dried fish
- 4 tablespoons ground crayfish

Vegetables:

- 1 ripe pumpkin
- 1 medium tomato, chopped
- 1 medium onion, chopped
- 2 fresh tatashe peppers, chopped
- 1 red bell pepper, chopped
- 1 bunch spinach, sliced
- 1 bunch sorrel leaves, chopped

3 or 4 bouillon cubes

Salt to taste

1 tablespoon locust bean spice

4 tablespoons palm oil

2 cups groundnuts (peanuts)

PREPARATION

- Cut pumpkin in half, peel the outer shell, and remove the seeds and hairy pulp. Cut pumpkin into chunks.
- In a large pot, place the various meats and fish, along with bouillon cubes and salt, with enough water to cover the meat.
- Once pumpkin is tender, use the back of a spoon and mash the chunks, leaving some bits that are not mashed.
- Slightly roast groundnuts in a pan. Then place groundnuts in a blender with 2 cups of water and blend until it forms a paste. (Alternatively, you can use 2 cups of pure groundnut butter.)
- Combine 2 cups of water, tomatoes, onions, peppers, and red bell peppers in a blender and blend. Transfer this mixture to a pot and heat it to remove most of the water content.
- Transfer the meat back to the pot with the pumpkin and cook until meat is done.
- Lower the heat a little, and gradually add groundnut paste, making sure it mixes smoothly into the soup mixture to avoid creating lumps and burning the soup. Add locust bean spice, tomatoes-pepper blend, and palm oil.
- Boil the soup for several minutes and then add the chopped spinach, and a few minutes later, the chopped sorrel leaves. The spinach leaves act as a garnish to the soup, while the sorrel leaves add a souring, tangy taste, providing a unique flavor to the soup.
- Let the vegetables simmer for 5 to 8 minutes and remove from heat. Check the seasoning and serve with fufu.

Groundnut Soup

Groundnut soup is loved all throughout West African countries: Ghana, Nigeria, Senegal, Gambia, and Mali. Groundnut soup has many names, such as “maffe,” “sauce d’arachide,” “tigadeguena,” or “domoda.”

Serves 8 to 10

INGREDIENTS

2 to 6 cups assorted meats and/or seafood:

- Goat meat
- Beef (tripe, shaki, pomo)
- Chicken
- 1 medium dried fish
- 3 tablespoons ground crayfish

Vegetables:

- 1 medium onion, sliced
- 2 fresh tomatoes, chopped
- 2 cups groundnuts
- 1 bunch green vegetables of choice

4 bouillon cubes, divided
Salt to taste
2 tablespoons freshly ground pepper
1 tablespoon locust bean spice
4 tablespoons palm oil

PREPARATION

- Wash and boil meat (except tripe, which is cooked in a separate step later). Add sliced onions, 2 bouillon cubes, and salt. Boil until meat is tender.
- Blend ground crayfish, tomatoes, and freshly ground pepper and set aside.
- Debone and wash dried fish with warm water and add to boiling meat. Add locust bean spice and crayfish-tomato-pepper blend to the pot.
- Roast groundnuts in a pan, constantly stirring. When their color turns to a golden brown, remove them from the pan and grind them into a powder.
- Wash and cut vegetables and set them aside.
- Cook beef tripe in just enough water to cover it. Add water periodically, but always just to the level that it covers the contents of the pot. When beef tripe begins to curl, add the fish. When the beef tripe is soft enough, add the chicken and/or beef or goat meat, as well as 2 bouillon cubes. Add crayfish-tomato-pepper blend to the pot. Cover the pot and allow the mixture to boil.
- Remove meat and fish from the pot and put them in a separate container. Reduce the heat to low and stir in the milled groundnuts. Allow the mixture to boil gently, stirring to prevent creating lumps and burning the groundnuts. Add palm oil and mix it thoroughly with the contents of the pot. Add water periodically.
- Transfer the meat and fish back to the pot and continue cooking on low heat. Now, add your choice of vegetable to the soup. Allow it to simmer for about 5 minutes. The soup is ready. Check the seasoning and serve with fufu.

Conclusion

Fufu is more than an art—more than a food. It's a symbol of West African culture. And the soups that accompany it each have a lineage and story of their own. When you eat fufu and soup, you're stepping into history and experiencing a rich cultural heritage. You've also learned about the nuances related to fufu, like eating with your hands, serving it with a plate and a bowl, and making room for trial and error.

As you have learned more about fufu, you have discovered a cultural treasure—the tapestry of the various peoples who have woven their lives and stories together to create a cultural masterpiece. Mold your world into a more inclusive place through this wonderful dish. That's the Art of Fufu.

And this is only the beginning. You'll find useful information in the following Appendices. For more recipes, go to TheArtofFufu.com. There's a whole world waiting for you to explore. Let my recipes be your tour guides.

Appendix A

Main Ingredients and How to Store Them

Store the following ingredients in a jar:

- Bouillon cubes: Many brands of bouillon cubes can be bought in any convenience store. They are small cubes of about one centimeter wrapped in light foil. They are made from natural spices mixed with some synthetic elements.
- Crayfish: This is bought in the market and usually consists of small dried fish and crabs.
- Dried pepper: See page 17.
- Dried prawns: Prawns are dried by putting them in the sun for a considerable amount of time. They are usually found in the Niger Delta region of Nigeria.
- Melon seeds: These are also generally referred to as "egusi" (refer to page 13 for a full description).
- Onga: This is processed locust bean spice, usually available in small packets that can be bought in any a specialty food market.

- Ogbono seeds: These seeds are harvested from the tree called the wild mango, African mango, or bush mango, with the botanical name *Irvingia gabonensis*. After the fruit is eaten, the seed is dried and used for soup.
- Potash: Potash is frequently used in the cooking process. Manufactured locally, it is made from plant ashes that are hardened into cubes and are water-soluble. In the olden days, this process was conducted in a pot, which is where it got its name.
- Uda: This is also known as negro pepper or Ethiopian pepper. It is very spicy and was used as a contraceptive in the olden days, according to word-of-mouth tales from elders. Its botanical name is *Xylopia aethiopica*.
- Uziza: The leaves and berries of the uziza plant are both used in African cuisine. The fresh leaves are pale green in color and have a peppery flavor. Its botanical name is *Piper guineense*.

Store the following ingredients in a cool, dry place:

- Cocoyam
- Plantains
- Rice
- Water yams

Store the following ingredients in the freezer:

- Smoked fish
- Stockfish

Store the following ingredients in the fridge:

- Periwinkle prawns (in a bowl of water)

Appendix B

Kitchen Equipment

The following pieces of kitchen equipment are used to make soup and fufu:

- Large wooden spoon for turning and scooping soup
- Small spoons for measuring spices
- Stainless steel baskets for straining and sieving
- Shredding knife
- Wooden spatula
- Mortar and pestle for pounding fufu
- Pots of various sizes
- Heat source (wood fire, gas cooker, charcoal stove, kerosene stove, sawdust stove)

> “A moment of love and fun expressed through collaboration and sharing on the platform of food.”
>
> **–Ogor**

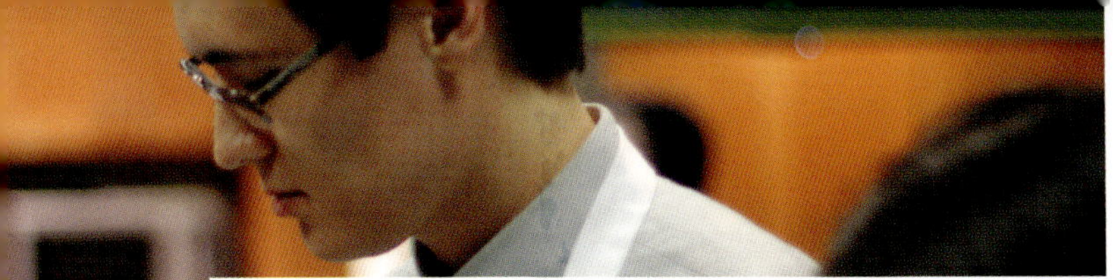

Appendix C

Testimonials

We hope you have enjoyed this introduction to fufu and the many soups that accompany it. We also want you to know that the Art of Fufu has been a delightful discovery for many others. Be sure to review the following testimonies that have come from other readers and Art of Fufu followers like you.

Cooking Class

> "The location was perfect and easy to find. The teacher was very kind, patient, and upbeat. She took time to even explain the culture behind the items we were cooking. I honestly enjoyed the whole experience immensely–cooking, wine, good music, and fellowshipping with others interested in the culture."
>
> **–Jane Udoewa**

Art of Fufu Show

“I can remember showing up to a venue I had never been to before and not knowing what to expect even though I had grown up my whole life eating fufu! I walked in and felt like I was in another world—the vibe, the live DJ, the fresh smell of outdoors, so many cultures eagerly awaiting to learn the Art of Fufu. Then I walked into the gallery and was *blown away*. The pictures, sculptures, and paintings were amazing. The colors and the angels that were captured were so lifelike. I definitely cannot wait for this event to happen again.”

—Jane Udoewa

“I enjoyed the Art of Fufu art show. It was great to network with a purpose—learning more about fufu and what goes with it. I'm Nigerian, so I have a good working (or shall we say eating) knowledge of fufu. But at Art of Fufu, I was able to try out types I've not eaten in the past with soups I've not had before. I actually discovered oat fufu! The displays of African food in beautiful ways was also pretty cool.”

—Abby Kotun

“A breath-taking display of audacity of the Nigerian spirit and courage, against the odds.”

—Ogor

Index

A

Abak Atama Soup, 76–77
acha, 36
Afang Soup, 46–47
African basil, 13
African mango seeds, 13
African nutmeg, 9
African walking catfish, 5
Agushi, 56–57
akamo, 36–37
alligator pepper, 17
amala fufu, 30, 37
añara, 12
Aridan fruit, 10
ataeko, 17
atama leaf, 11
Abak Atama Soup, 76–77
atare, 17
ata rodo pepper, 19

B

Banga Soup, 74–75
baobab leaves, 84–85
basil, 78–79
beans
- Gbegiri soup, 70–71
- locust, 9, 10

beef
- Abak Atama Soup, 76–77
- Afang Soup, 46–47
- Banga Soup, 74–75
- Bitter Leaf Soup, 52–53
- Edikang Ikong Soup, 44–45
- Egusi Soup, 56–57
- Garden Egg Leaf Soup, 54–55
- general discussion, 2
- Groundnut soup, 88–89
- Miyan Kuka, 84–85
- Miyan Taushe, 86–87
- Nsala Soup, 80–81
- Obe Efo Riro, 68–69
- Ofe Oha, 50–51
- Ofe Owerri, 48–49
- Ogbono Soup, 62–63
- Okra Soup, 60–61
- tenderness of, 4

big black snail, 7
bitter leaf
- Banga Soup, 74–75
- Bitter Leaf Soup, 52–53
- Egusi Soup, 56–57
- general discussion, 11
- Ogbono Soup, 62–63

Bitter Leaf Soup, 52–53
bonga fish, 5
bouillon cubes, 9, 93

C

Calabash nutmeg, 9
cassava
  cassava fufu, 24–26, 38
  garri fufu, 26, 27
  overview, 23, 37
cassava fufu, 24–26
catfish
  general discussion, 5
  Nsala Soup, 80–81
  smoked, 7
chicken
  general discussion, 3, 4
  Groundnut soup, 88–89
  Miyan Kuka, 84–85
  Miyan Taushe, 86–87
cocoyam, 95
cocoyam fufu, 31
codfish, 8
corn flour fufu, 36–37
cows, 2
crabs, 5
crayfish, 5, 93

D

dikka nuts, 13
domoda, 88–89
draw soups
  Ogbono Soup, 62–63
  Okra Soup, 60–61
dried fish, 5–6

E

eating fufu, 22, 39–41
eba meal, 22
Edikang Ikong Soup, 44–45
Efik people, 56–57
egusi, 13
Egusi Soup, 56–57
ehuru seeds, 9
elubo, 30
Eru, 46–47
Ethiopian pepper, 94
etiquette, fufu, 39–41
ewedu leaf, 12
  Ewedu Soup, 12

F

fermented cassava, 24–25
fish
  Abak Atama Soup, 76–77
  Afang Soup, 46–47
  Banga Soup, 74–75
  Bitter Leaf Soup, 52–53
  catfish, 5, 7
  dried, 5–6
  Edikang Ikong Soup, 44–45
  Egusi Soup, 56–57
  Fisherman Soup, 78–79
  Garden Egg Leaf Soup, 54–55
  Groundnut soup, 88–89
  mackerel, 6, 7
  Miyan Kuka, 84–85
  Miyan Taushe, 86–87
  Nsala Soup, 80–81
  Obe Efo Riro, 68–69
  Ofe Oha, 50–51
  Ofe Owerri, 48–49
  Ogbono Soup, 62–63
  Okra Soup, 60–61
  smoked, 4, 7
  stockfish, 8
  storing, 95
Fisherman Soup, 78–79
flour
  corn, 36–37
  plantain, 33
  wheat, 34
  yam, 29–30
fonio, 36

forks and knives, eating fufu with, 39–40
fufu etiquette, 39–41
fufu ingredients
  cassava
    cassava fufu, 24–26
    garri, 26
    garri fufu, 27
    overview, 23, 37
  cocoyam, 31
  grains
    tuwo, 35–37
    tuwo acha, 36
    tuwo masara, 36–37
    tuwo shinkafa, 35–36
    wheat flour, 34
  overview, 22
  plantain, 32, 37
  plantain flour, 33
  semolina, 34
  yams
    amala fufu, 30, 37
    overview, 28
    yam flour fufu, 29–30
    yam fufu, 37

G

GALS (giant African land snail), 7
garden egg leaves, 12
  Garden Egg Leaf Soup, 54–55
garri fufu, 26, 27
Gbegiri soup, 70–71
Ghana tiger snail, 7
giant African land snail (GALS), 7
goat
  Abak Atama Soup, 76–77
  Afang Soup, 46–47
  Banga Soup, 74–75
  Bitter Leaf Soup, 52–53
  Edikang Ikong Soup, 44–45
  Egusi Soup, 56–57
  Garden Egg Leaf Soup, 54–55
  general discussion, 3
  Groundnut soup, 88–89
  Miyan Kuka, 84–85
  Miyan Taushe, 86–87
  Nsala Soup, 80–81
  Obe Efo Riro, 68–69
  Ofe Oha, 50–51
  Ofe Owerri, 48–49
  Ogbono Soup, 62–63
  Okra Soup, 60–61
  tenderness of, 4
grains
  tuwo, 35–37
  tuwo acha, 36
  tuwo masara, 36–37
  tuwo shinkafa, 35–36
  wheat flour, 34
groundnuts
  Groundnut soup, 88–89
  Miyan Taushe, 86–87
ground red pepper, 17

H

hands, washing, 39–41
hens
  Abak Atama Soup, 76–77
  Afang soup, 46–47
  Banga Soup, 74–75
  Edikang Ikong Soup, 44–45
  Egusi Soup, 56–57
  general discussion, 3
  Nsala Soup, 80–81
  Obe Efo Riro, 68–69
  Ofe añara, 54–55
  Ofe Owerri, 48–49
  Ogbono Soup, 62–63
  Okra Soup, 60–61
herring fish, 5–6
hungry man rice, 36

I

ikong-ubong, 14
ingredients
- in fufu
  - cassava, 23–27, 37
  - cocoyam, 31
  - overview, 22
  - plantain, 32, 37
  - plantain flour, 33
  - semolina, 34
  - tuwo, 35–37
  - wheat flour, 34
  - yams, 28–30, 37
- meats
  - beef, 2
  - goat, 3
  - poultry, 3
  - tenderness of, 4
- palm oil, 1
- peppers
  - alligator pepper, 17
  - ground red pepper, 17
  - negro pepper, 18, 94
  - red bell pepper, 18
  - Scotch bonnet pepper, 19
- seafood
  - catfish, 5
  - crabs, 5
  - crayfish, 5, 93
  - dried fish, 5–6
  - mackerel, 6
  - overview, 4
  - periwinkles, 6
  - prawns and shrimp, 7, 93
  - smoked fish, 7
  - snails, 7
  - stockfish, 8
- seasonings
  - bouillon cubes, 9, 93
  - ehuru seeds, 9
  - locust beans, 9, 10
  - potash, 10, 94
  - uyakay, 10
- storing, 93–95
- vegetables
  - Atama leaf, 11
  - bitter leaf, 11
  - ewedu leaf, 12
  - garden egg leaves, 12
  - melon seeds, 13, 93
  - Nchuanwu leaf, 13
  - ogbono seed, 13, 94
  - oha leaf, 12
  - onga, 93
  - Palm nuts and palm fruit, 14
  - pumpkin leaves, 14
  - ukazi leaf, 14
  - utazi leaf, 15
  - uziza leaf, 16
  - waterleaf, 15

J

Jamaican nutmeg, 9
jute leaves, 12
- Ewedu Soup, 66–67

K

kitchen equipment, 97
Kotun, Abby, 101
kuka, 84–85

L

leaves
- atama, 11, 76–77
- baobab, 84–85
- bitter
  - Banga Soup, 74–75
  - Bitter Leaf Soup, 52–53
  - Egusi Soup, 56–57
  - general discussion, 11
  - Ogbono Soup, 62–63

ewedu, 12
garden egg, 12, 54–55
jute, 12, 66–67
Nchuanwu, 13
oha, 12, 50–51
okazi, 14, 56–57
ora, 12
pumpkin
Edikang Ikong Soup, 44–45
Egusi Soup, 56–57
Fisherman Soup, 78–79
general discussion, 14
Ofe Owerri, 48–49
Ogbono Soup, 62–63
Okra Soup, 60–61
sorrel, 86–87
ukazi
Afang Soup, 46–47
Egusi Soup, 56–57
general discussion, 14
Ofe Owerri, 48–49
utazi, 15
uziza, 16, 80–81, 94
waterleaf, 15, 44–45, 46–47
locust beans, 9, 10
Luru Soup, 84–85

M

mackerel, 6, 7
maffe, 88–89
meats
Abak Atama Soup, 76–77
Afang Soup, 46–47
Banga Soup, 74–75
beef, 2
Bitter Leaf Soup, 52–53
Edikang Ikong Soup, 44–45
Egusi Soup, 56–57
Garden Egg Leaf Soup, 54–55
goat, 3
Groundnut soup, 88–89
Miyan Kuka, 84–85
Miyan Taushe, 86–87
Nsala Soup, 80–81
Obe Efo Riro, 68–69
Ofe Oha, 50–51
Ofe Owerri, 48–49
Ogbono Soup, 62–63
Okra Soup, 60–61
poultry, 3
tenderness of, 4
melon seeds, 13, 93
Miyan Gushi, 56–57
Miyan Kuka, 84–85
Miyan Taushe, 86–87

N

Nchuanwu leaf, 13
negro pepper, 18, 94
Niger Delta specialties
Abak Atama Soup, 76–77
Banga Soup, 74–75
Fisherman Soup, 78–79
Nsala Soup, 80–81
Nigerian Dwarf goat, 3
Northern Nigerian specialties
Groundnut soup, 88–89
Miyan Kuka, 84–85
Miyan Taushe, 86–87
Nsala Soup, 80–81
nutmeg, African, 9

O

Obe Efo Elegusi, 56–57
Obe Efo Riro, 68–69
Ofe añara, 55–56
Ofe Oha, 50–51
Ofe Owerri, 48–49
ogbono seed
general discussion, 13
health benefits of, 62
Ogbono Soup, 62–63

Okra Soup, 60–61
storing, 94
Ogbono Soup, 62–63
Ogor, 101
oha leaf, 12
Ofe Oha, 50–51
okazi leaf, 14
Egusi Soup, 56–57
okra
Fisherman Soup, 78–79
Miyan Kuka, 84–85
Okra Soup, 60–61
onga, 93
ora leaf, 12

P

Palm nuts and palm fruit, 14
palm oil, 1
pap, 36–37
peppers
alligator, 17
ground red, 17
negro, 18, 94
red bell, 18
Scotch bonnet, 19
periwinkles, 6, 95
pilipili-hoho, 18
plantains, 95
plantain flour, 33
plantain fufu, 32, 37
pomo, 2
potash, 10, 94
poultry, 3
pounded fufu, making from scratch, 38
prawns, 7, 93
pumpkin, 86–87
pumpkin leaves
Edikang Ikong Soup, 44–45
Egusi Soup, 56–57
Fisherman Soup, 78–79
general discussion, 14
Ofe Owerri, 48–49
Ogbono Soup, 62–63
Okra Soup, 60–61

R

red bell pepper, 18
rice fufu, 35–36
rice, storing, 95
rolling fufu, 40

S

sauce d'arachide, 88–89
Scotch bonnet pepper, 19
seafood
Abak Atama Soup, 76–77
Afang Soup, 46–47
Banga Soup, 74–75
Bitter Leaf Soup, 52–53
catfish, 5
crabs, 5
crayfish, 5, 93
dried fish, 5–6
Edikang Ikong Soup, 44–45
Egusi Soup, 56–57
Fisherman Soup, 78–79
Garden Egg Leaf Soup, 54–55
Groundnut soup, 88–89
mackerel, 6
Miyan Kuka, 84–85
Miyan Taushe, 86–87
Nsala Soup, 80–81
Obe Efo Riro, 68–69
Ofe Oha, 50–51
Ofe Owerri, 48–49
Ogbono Soup, 62–63
Okra Soup, 60–61
overview, 4
periwinkles, 6
prawns and shrimp, 7, 93
smoked fish, 7
snails, 7

stockfish, 8
seasonings
bouillon cubes, 9, 93
ehuru seeds, 9
locust beans, 9, 10
potash, 10, 94
uyakay, 10
seeds
African mango, 13
ehuru, 9
melon, 13, 93
ogbono
general discussion, 13
health benefits of, 62
Ogbono Soup, 62–63
Okra Soup, 60–61
storing, 94
semolina fufu, 34
Senegal pepper, 18
shaki, 2
shawa, 5
shrimp, 7
smoked fish, 4, 7, 95
snails, 7
sorrel leaf, 86–87
soups
draw
Ogbono Soup, 62–63
Okra Soup, 60–61
Niger Delta
Abak Atama Soup, 76–77
Banga Soup, 74–75
Fisherman Soup, 78–79
Nsala Soup, 80–81
Northern Nigerian
Groundnut soup, 88–89
Miyan Kuka, 84–85
Miyan Taushe, 86–87
vegetable
Afang Soup, 46–47
Bitter Leaf Soup, 52–53
Edikang Ikong Soup, 44–45
Egusi Soup, 56–57
Garden Egg Leaf Soup, 54–55
Ofe Oha, 50–51
Ofe Owerri, 48–49
Western Nigerian
Ewedu Soup, 66–67
Gbegiri soup, 70–71
Obe Efo Riro, 68–69
spinach
Miyan Taushe, 86–87
Obe Efo Riro, 68–69
stockfish, 8, 95
swallow meal, 22

T

tatashe, 18
testimonials, 99–101
tigadeguena, 88–89
Titus fish, 6
tripe
beef, 2
goat, 3
turkey, 3, 4
tuwo, 35–37
tuwo acha, 36
tuwo masara, 36–37
tuwo shinkafa, 35–36

U

uda, 18, 94
Udoewa, Jane, 99, 100
ugu, 14
ukazi leaf
Afang Soup, 46–47
Egusi Soup, 56–57
general discussion, 14
Ofe Owerri, 48–49
utazi leaf, 15
uyakay, 10
uziza leaf
general discussion, 16

Nsala Soup, 80–81
storing, 94

V

vegetables
Atama leaf, 11
bitter leaf, 11
ewedu leaf, 12
garden egg leaves, 12
melon seeds, 13, 93
Nchuanwu leaf, 13
ogbono seed, 13, 94
oha leaf, 12
onga, 93
Palm nuts and palm fruit, 14
pumpkin leaves, 14
ukazi leaf, 14
utazi leaf, 15
uziza leaf, 16
waterleaf, 15
vegetable soups
Afang Soup, 46–47
Bitter Leaf Soup, 52–53
Edikang Ikong Soup, 44–45
Egusi Soup, 56–57
Garden Egg Leaf Soup, 54–55
Ofe Oha, 50–51
Ofe Owerri, 48–49

W

washing hands, 39–41
waterleaf
Afang Soup, 46–47
Edikang Ikong Soup, 44–45
general discussion, 15
West African Mud Creepers, 6
Western Nigerian specialties
Ewedu Soup, 66–67
Gbegiri soup, 70–71
Obe Efo Riro, 68–69
wheat flour, 34
whentia, 18
White Soup, 80–81

Y

yams
amala fufu, 30, 37
Nsala Soup, 80–81
overview, 28

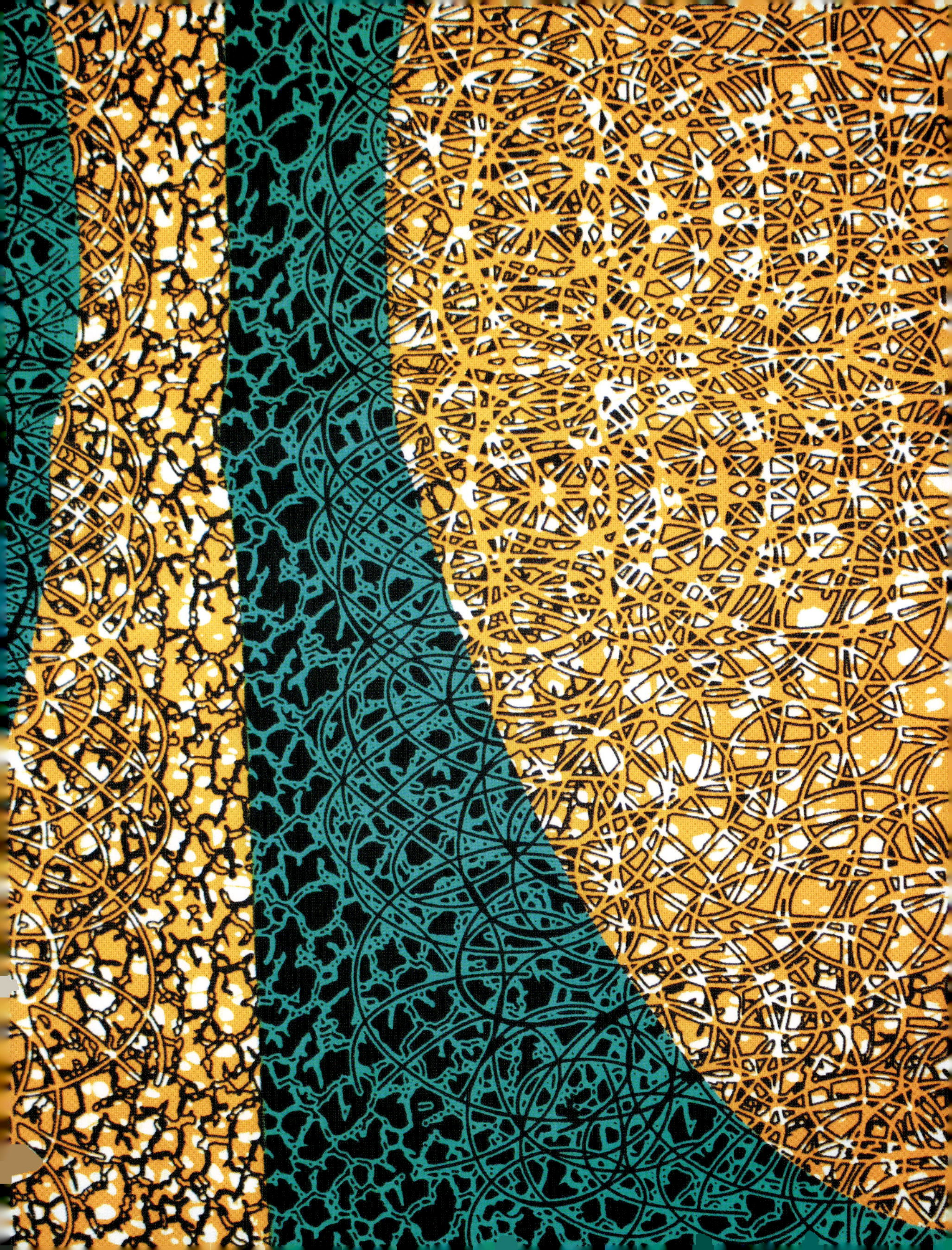

THE
ART
OF
FUFU®

About

TheArtofFufu.com

Our long-term vision is to give fufu a place among the world's finest culinary traditions. Through this book, *The Art of Fufu*, and our website, TheArtofFufu.com, we seek to fulfill our vision and offer a stunning, full-color experience that gives readers a better understanding of fufu, its cultural history, and its traditional flair. An intimate journey into typical West African kitchens, the book and website will give readers insight into the region's deep cultural roots. Providing guidance, starting with table etiquette, each chapter in *The Art of Fufu* peers more deeply into this breathtaking region and its culinary diversity. Our vision is to impact lives through breaking barriers and uniting all of us on a plate. Come and roll some fufu with us! Visit our website today!

About the Author

FROM THE TIME she was a child, global food ambassador Kavachi Michelle Ukegbu has had a passion for bringing people together through good food for stronger cultural connections. That passion came to full fruition when she founded Grubido.com, a website whose mission is to expand international food awareness. Through Grubido, Kavachi fuses her training in the culinary arts, marketing, and hospitality management to host enriching in-person experiences crafted to expand guests' culinary horizons. Grubido conducts art shows, called "The Art of Fufu," throughout the greater Houston area. These shows feature food, beverage tastings, classes, West African culture, works of art, and music—all fulfilling her mission to spread the love of international food to those who haven't ventured outside their cultural bubble.

A third-generation culinary professional with Nigerian heritage, Kavachi spent her formative years cultivating a passion for food in her mother's restaurant, Safari, the first and longest-running African restaurant in Houston. Inspired by her mother and eager to build on her legacy, Kavachi embarked on her academic journey. She broadened her perspective and explored the finer points of business and dining at Università Bocconi in Milan, Italy.

Upon returning to Houston, Kavachi attracted attention quickly with her first venture, the Peppersoup Cafe, earning glowing reviews from renowned Houston food critics Katharine Shilcutt and Allison Cook. Despite her early success, Kavachi's vision for new creative concepts led her to suspend operations at Peppersoup and return to school, honing her cooking skills and her business acumen at the University of Houston's Hilton College of Hotel and Restaurant Management.

In 2013, Kavachi launched Grubido, a first-of-its-kind movement to take international culinary concepts to the mainstream. A far cry from a traditional restaurant group, Grubido is a movement—a rallying cry for food lovers to expand their palates and discover global cuisine through local food-tasting events, interactive web content, and more.